THE
PASTA
MAKER
BIBLE

Unveil the Secrets of Dough and Shapes, Dive into
Foolproof Recipes, and Celebrate Homemade Pasta with
Loved Ones

DIANE ROMANO

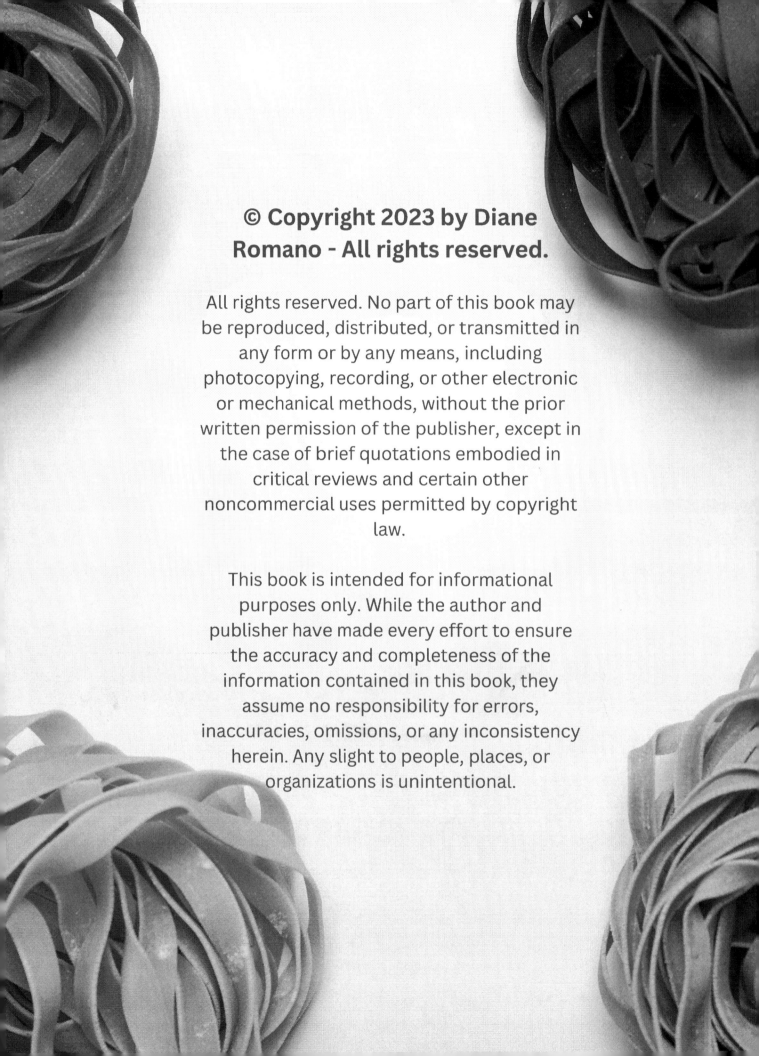

CONTENTS

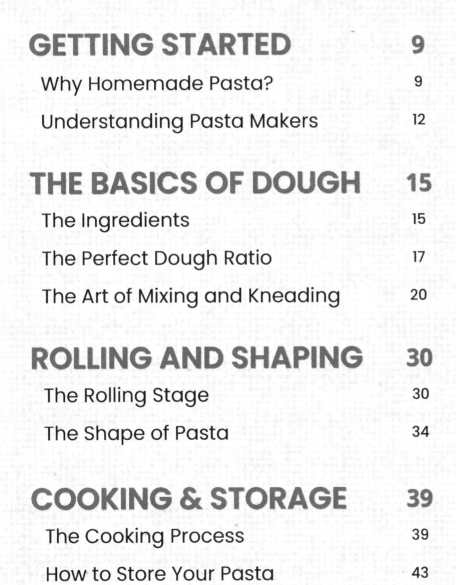

PART II: RECIPE JOURNEY

2 EXCLUSiVE FREE BONUSES FOR YOU!

Don't forget to download them

Jump Now To the End of the Book
and scan the QR code!

INTRODUCTION

Hey there, foodies! Welcome to a culinary adventure that's steeped in the history of Italy's gorgeous landscapes yet as fresh as basil leaves plucked straight from grandma's herb garden.

You're here because you've scored yourself an awesome pasta maker, and you can't wait to turn humble ingredients into drool-worthy meals that comfort the soul. Good news, you're exactly where you need to be.

I'm an Italian-American grandmother who loves embracing my rich cultural traditions. I've invested all my passion and creativity into this book. It's not just another recipe collection gathering dust on your kitchen shelf.

Instead, it's your go-to guide for everything related to pasta-making; getting under the skin of your new gadget, mastering dough like a pro, learning about countless pasta shapes or understanding how sauces can magically transform dishes, the works!

But we're not stopping at recipes, we'll delve into heartwarming stories behind each dish; traditions passed down through generations; handy tips and hacks all adding up to make eating more than just food consumption but truly an experience.

This is the culmination of my culinary journey, years spent sweating over a hot stove. I'm genuinely stoked to give you a peek into it.

The beauty of pasta? It's like your favorite pair of jeans - dress it up for a night out or keep it casual for chilling at home. Feel free to stick with timeless favorites or dare yourself with funky combinations. The options are limitless and that's what this book aims to explore.

So, ready to get down and doughy? Let's dive headfirst into this mouthwatering adventure together because life is all about mixing magic and macaroni. And let's face it, who couldn't use an extra sprinkle of enchantment in their lives?

Part 01

PASTA MAKER 101

Alright, folks, let's dive headfirst into the epic adventure of pasta making. Central to this edible art form is our trusty sidekick - the pasta maker! This nifty gadget acts as a bridge between humble ingredients and finger-licking dishes.

In this section, we'll get up close and personal with homemade pasta, a celebration of its mouthwatering flavors, satisfying textures, and the sheer happiness it brings to meal times. We'll take a closer look at the two main types of pasta makers, each with their own set of bells and whistles that make them stand out in their own unique way.

But wait...our voyage isn't over yet; we're going deep into dough territory too! From choosing top-notch ingredients to mastering kneading and rolling like an Italian nonna. And as we progress, I'll share insights on shaping pasta, ensuring that each type, be it fettuccine or ravioli, is crafted to perfection.

We won't leave any stone unturned, we're also talking cooking tips for that oh-so-perfect al dente bite along with smart storage hacks so you don't have to say goodbye to leftovers!

Drawing inspiration from an old-school Italian-American grandma who knew her stuff when it came down to traditional cuisine. This section promises one helluva gastronomic journey filled with expertise rooted in love.

So, with anticipation in our hearts, let's dive into the world of pasta-making together.

WHY HOMEMADE PASTA?

You might be scratching your head and asking, "Why on earth would I bother making pasta from scratch when I can just yoink a box off the supermarket shelf?" Well, allow me to let you in on some family wisdom. Whipping up homemade pasta isn't merely about cooking; it's an engaging journey that stirs your soul and excites your taste buds in ways pre-packaged noodles simply can't compete with. In this segment, we're going deep into the many benefits of DIY pasta - from its health boons to how its flavour profile and mouthfeel totally outshine ready-made options.

The Benefits of Homemade Pasta

Let's dive into something I totally love: the absolute bliss and perks of whipping up your own pasta at home. Man, the scent of fresh dough you've kneaded yourself, the hands-on fun of rolling it out, and that awesome feeling when you see those strands or sheets take form!

- **Taste Superiority:** In the age of convenience, it's all too easy to reach for store-bought pasta. But when you make your own homemade version, there are so many flavor possibilities! Fresh eggs and flour make a world of difference; no preservatives mean the pure Italian flavors can really shine through. Each bite will be like an explosion of taste in your mouth; there's nothing like it compared to pre-packaged options. If you're looking for something truly special, making fresh pasta is definitely worth giving a try!

- **Texture Customization:** The texture of homemade noodles is really exciting! As the head chef, you can customize your noodles to be as chewy or soft as you wish. Do you want it al dente with a little bite? Or do you prefer it softer and ready to absorb all the goodness of the sauce? It's all up to you: you can determine the dough time, the thickness of the sheet and the length of time it is baked until it meets your standards of perfection. There is nothing better than homemade pasta when you have control over every step of the process!

- **Ingredient Control:** When it comes to ingredients, there's nothing better than having full control over what goes into your food. In an age where dietary restrictions and allergies have become the norm rather than the exception, being able to handpick each ingredient is a major plus. Want gluten-free flour or eggs from free-range chickens? No problem! Feeling bold enough for some spinach juice in your pasta? Go ahead! The possibilities are endless. And the best part: there's zero chance of any artificial flavors or preservatives sneaking their way onto your plate; you're keeping things 100% natural - just how nature intended it.

- **Nutritional Benefits:** Whipping up your own pasta is a game changer. You're keeping all the stellar stuff: proteins, vitamins, and minerals from the eggs and flour intact. It's like fueling your body with pure goodness while also catering to your taste buds - top-notch stealth health move for sure!

- **The Joy of Creation:** Seriously though, there's this unadulterated satisfaction in getting hands-on. Kneading that dough till it's just right, rolling it out into perfect thinness and chopping it into shapes you love, feels almost therapeutic! This labor of love isn't just about filling bellies but about putting smiles on faces too, it's an achievement badge worth flaunting! And those grinning faces around the dinner table? That's just icing on the cake!

Health Advantages

- **No Preservatives or Additives:** with homemade pasta, there are zero unknown elements or chemical preservatives lurking around - perfect for those with food allergies or sensitivities. It gives you a clean canvas to create your culinary art without worrying about any potential harmful stuff messing with your body.

- **Nutrient Retention:** the nutrient-rich profile of homemade pasta easily trumps what you get from store shelves, which often lose nutrients during production and drying processes. Cooking up some fresh dough at home ensures the nutritional value stays intact – protein rich eggs and fiber-loaded flour make for a tasty yet healthy treat- an absolute win-win!

- **Dietary Flexibility:** got specific dietary needs? Fret not! Homemade pasta is like your personal diet fairy godmother. Need gluten-free? Swap regular flour with gluten-free alternatives; following veganism? Ditch eggs for plant-based substitutes. You have control over every single ingredient going into your dish making sure it fits perfectly within your dietary boundaries – just like a tailor-made suit!

- **Lower Glycemic Index:** did you know whipping up your own pasta at home can be a game changer for your blood sugar levels? How cool is that! Home-made pasta usually has a lower glycemic index compared to the stuff you grab off the shelves. The secret lies in using high-quality, unprocessed ingredients which take longer for our body to break down. It's a small yet meaningful hack towards maintaining our long-term health.

- **Mental Health Benefits:** let's not overlook the mental health benefits of making pasta from scratch. The act of creating something with your own hands is incredibly therapeutic. The repetitive motions of kneading and can be meditative, helping to reduce stress and anxiety. It's not just about feeding your body; it's about nourishing your soul.

- **Freshness Factor:** freshly made = nutrient-packed goodness - period! By making your own pasta at home, you're quite literally serving yourself an extra dose of health benefits right on the plate. Imagine biting into an apple picked straight from an orchard, that's what homemade meals feel like!

From the absence of preservatives to the joy of creation, each step of the pasta-making process offers its own set of health advantages. It's not just about eating; it's about living well. As we often say, "La salute viene mangiando", health comes through eating. And what better way to eat healthily than with pasta made by your own hands?

Flavor and Texture Comparison

Let me tell you, the distinction between homemade pasta and the stuff off-the-shelf isn't just about wellness. It's also about that rich taste and unique texture only your own kitchen can whip up.

- **Depth of Flavor:** homemade pasta packs a punch of flavor that is simply unrivaled. When crafting pasta from scratch, it's more than just eggs and flour - it's mixing in passion, heritage and top-notch ingredients. What do we get? A depth of flavor store-bought options can never live up to. The eggs bring a creamy richness; the flour adds subtle undertones while herbs or spices give an extra kick if you're keen on experimenting! It's like being at a concert with each ingredient working in unison to create this symphony for your palate.
- **Texture Versatility:** Herein lies the real magic, making your own pasta gives you total control over its texture right from step one till plating time! Craving something al dente? Done deal! More into softer noodles? Your wish is its command! From thickness to bite size down to chewiness, it's all within your reach! Want some variety? Try playing around with different flours- use semolina for a stiff bite or whole wheat for an earthy touch. You are practically shaping art out of dough here - Picasso style!
- The power truly rests with you when making homemade pasta compared to settling for generic store-bought variants. You're not restricted by what someone else thinks good pasta should be but rather given full freedom over every single detail which makes all the difference!
- **Freshness Impact:** fresh pasta absorbs sauces better, making each bite a perfect blend of all the ingredients. The freshness elevates the dish from a mere meal to an event, a celebration of sorts. It's the difference between a canned song on the radio and a live concert in your favorite venue: both can be enjoyable, but the latter is an experience.
- **Culinary Creativity:** the creative freedom you have with homemade pasta is a flavor and texture advantage in itself. Want to infuse your pasta with spinach, beetroot, or squid ink for added flavor and color? Go ahead! Feel like experimenting with shapes and sizes? The world is your oyster, or in this case, your pasta bowl. This creative license allows you to tailor the dish to your personal preferences, making each meal a unique culinary adventure.

UNDERSTANDING PASTA MAKERS

Let's hit pause and get to know the heart of our pasta-making journey: the pasta maker itself. This nifty device is not just another kitchen gadget; it's your ticket to transforming basic ingredients into a culinary masterpiece.

Brief Overview of What a Pasta Maker Is and Its Basic Functions

A pasta maker is essentially your sidekick in the realm of homemade pasta creation. It's like having an extra pair of hands in the kitchen, dedicated solely to crafting the perfect pasta. But what exactly does it do, and how does it work? Let's explore.

Think of a pasta maker as your personal sous-chef for all things noodle-related. It has two main gigs: turning dough into sheets and then slicing them up into beautiful shapes. The rolling part basically takes your carefully kneaded dough ball, which you put so much love (and elbow grease) into, flattens it down with precision that would leave any rolling pin green with envy. After getting those sheets at just-the-right-thickness, comes its second act: cutting! Here we go from flat sheet to gorgeous strands or ribbons, whether spaghetti or fettuccine, or whatever tickles your fancy.

But the pasta party doesn't stop there. Today's pasta machines come with customizable settings that let you play around with your pasta thickness. Craving those thin sheets for ravioli or are we going hearty like pappardelle? Many pasta makers offer a variety of attachments designed for crafting different pasta shapes. These attachments are like your personal pasta shape-shifters, each designed to create a specific type of pasta. Simply switch out the attachment, and voila, you're ready to explore new culinary territories.

Now, let's talk about how these marvelous machines operate. There are different types of mechanisms to suit your level of involvement in the pasta-making process. The traditional pasta makers are manual, operated by a hand-crank. You feed the dough through the rollers by turning the crank, offering you a level of control that some find meditative. Then there are manual pasta makers with an added motor, offering a bit of automation without completely taking your hands out of the process. And let's not forget the popular KitchenAid attachment, which turns your stand mixer into a pasta-making powerhouse. While this option offers the utmost convenience, it does take away some of the tactile joy that comes with hand-cranking.

What Pasta Maker Can Do

Let's dive into the culinary magic this epic pasta maker can whip up in your kitchen. Believe me, it's not just about spaghetti or fettuccine; the sky's literally the limit.

First off, let's touch base with good old classics. A pasta maker effortlessly rolls out sheets for lasagna that are perfect enough to layer you straight into food heaven! Use those exact same sheets and voila - ravioli, tortellini, and other stuffed pastas at your disposal. Just slap on some filling – cheese? Meat? Veggies? You pick! Fold 'em over and cut them into whatever shape tickles your fancy. It's basically like owning a tiny Italian bakery within arm's reach!

But why stop there? With the right attachment, your pasta maker can churn out beautiful strands of spaghetti, fettucine, and capellini. These are the staples of Italian cuisine, and making them fresh elevates their flavors to a whole new level. Imagine twirling your fork into a plate of freshly made spaghetti, each strand absorbing the flavors of your sauce. It's a culinary experience that no store-bought pasta can match.

For those who enjoy wider and flatter noodles, a pasta maker can produce fettuccine, tagliatelle, and pappardelle. These are perfect when paired with robust sauces like Bolognese or Alfredo - their wide surface practically drinks up all that saucy goodness ensuring every bite is an explosion of flavor.

Now, for those who are health-conscious or have dietary restrictions, a pasta maker is a godsend. You get full control over what goes into your dough - whether it's gluten-free or whole-wheat – you call the shots! How about sneaking in some spinach or beetroot? Not only will this add nutritional value but also brighten up your plate!

Manual Pasta Maker vs. Attachment

When I first kicked off my pasta-making journey, it was with a manual machine: a precious gift from my Italian grandmother. She always said to me, "Honey, this machine will teach you patience and the sweet satisfaction of hard work." And boy, she wasn't kidding! The manual pasta maker is not just easy on your pocket but also convenient due to its portability. You can carry that bad boy wherever you want without needing a designated space on your kitchen counter.

Now, let's pause for a moment to consider the KitchenAid attachment. Ah, what a marvel of modern technology! A few years ago my children gave it to me for Christmas, saying it was time to "step into the future." And indeed, it's a game-changer. Unlike the manual pasta maker, which requires one hand to turn the crank, the KitchenAid attachment leaves both your hands free. Imagine the ease of handling long sheets of pasta without the juggle! Plus, there's no need to clamp it to a table, and you get to choose your rolling speed. The motor ensures a consistent speed, making your work much smoother.

However, let's not forget the investment involved. The attachment itself is a bit pricey, and if you don't already own a KitchenAid mixer, well, that's another considerable expense. So, who should go for what? If you're just starting your pasta-making journey, a manual machine is your best bet. It allows you to gauge how often you'll be making pasta before you decide to invest more. And here's a little secret: you can always add a motor to your manual machine later on!

On the other hand, if you're a seasoned pasta aficionado and already own a KitchenAid mixer, or plan to invest in one, the attachment is a fantastic choice. It's particularly useful for those who find themselves making pasta quite often and appreciate the extra convenience and features.

So here's the deal - deciding between a manual pasta maker or that shiny KitchenAid attachment comes down to your specific needs, your budget, and just how deep you've dived into this whole pasta-making gig. Each has their own perks depending on what scene you're in. Choose wisely, and you'll find that making pasta at home becomes not just a hobby, but a joyous way of life.

Cleaning and Maintenance Tips

Making pasta is a real treat, but like all brilliant things in life, it comes with its own set of duties. Yeah, I'm referring to the not-so-fun task of cleaning and taking care of your pasta maker. Believe me when I say that a little TLC can make sure this bad boy sticks around for the long haul.

Why's cleaning such a big deal? Well first off, it's about keeping things sanitary. Nobody wants crusty old bits of dough hanging out – hello bacteria party! But cleanliness isn't everything; we're talking about giving your machine an extended lifespan here. A well-cared-for pasta maker will be there by your side year after year - who knows maybe even decades!I still have the one my Nonna gave me, and it works like a charm, all thanks to regular upkeep.

Alright then, let's dive into some action now- how do you exactly clean this thing? Here are step-by-step Directions. on keeping your beloved pasta-making partner in tip-top shape:

- **Step 1:** make sure your pasta maker is bone dry before you even consider cleaning it. If you've got the dough right from the start, there shouldn't be any wet clumps sticking to your machine.
- **·Step 2:** lip that pasta maker upside down and give it a friendly tap. This should shake loose any dried-up bits of pasta. If your dough was a little on the damp side, some stubborn pieces might still hang around inside. But remember, water is not your friend here! Let 'em dry out completely – heck take all night if necessary- then get back to it.
- **Step 3:** next up, grab yourself a stiff bristle brush and lightly scrub away those pesky dried-out pasta chunks. If they've been sitting for at least an hour or so getting hard as rocks; they'll surrender without much fight.
- **Step 4:** for those really headstrong pieces that simply won't quit? A toothpick or skewer will do just fine. Just keep this in mind - no knives or sharp objects allowed! You definitely don't want to risk messing up your beloved machine.
- **Step 5:** Finally, to wrap things up, give that shiny piece of equipment, a good rubdown with a dry microfiber cloth. It'll have her looking brand spankin' new again.

Alright, let's dive into the maintenance of your pasta maker. Just like you'd give your car an oil change now and then, it's crucial to show some love to this kitchen gadget too by lubricating its gears with food-grade oil. This will have it running like a well-oiled machine, literally.

And while we're at that, eyeball those screws for any loose ends because trust me, a wobbly pasta maker is not on anyone's list of fun things. So if they seem shaky or undone over time, grab a screwdriver and tighten them up.

The storage, the final piece of the puzzle. You might think, "I'll just shove it in a cupboard and forget about it." But hold on a minute. Proper storage is essential to avoid rust and damage. Always store your pasta maker in a dry place. If it's a manual machine, detach the crank and the clamp for more compact storage. Keep them in the box they came in; it's designed to protect them.

Your pasta maker is not just a kitchen appliance; it's a gateway to delicious, homemade meals that bring the family together. It deserves respect and care. So next round when whipping out delicious noodles from scratch becomes tempting remember cleaning & maintaining are equally vital aspects (not unlike picking out top-notch ingredients themselves); making each serving truly special through all artistry & affection poured therein whilst preparing fresh hand-made pasta!

THE BASICS OF PASTA DOUGH

THE INGREDIENTS

Simple ingredients can whip up something truly amazing. But don't let their simplicity fool you; each ingredient adds its unique twist to the mix. So, let's dig into these culinary secrets!

Types of Flour and Their Properties

All flours aren't created equal – your choice of flour can be a game-changer for your pasta in terms of texture, taste, and even nutritional value. The star player here is protein content - aim for flour with around 9-13% protein because that's what develops enough gluten to make your pasta just right: chewy yet elastic! Too little protein might leave you with a limp noodle situation; too much could mean biting into a tough mess.

- **The Italian Grades: "00" and "0":** If you're a pasta connoisseur, then these are definitely your holy grail. These flours come finely ground, leaving your pasta with an unrivaled smoothness that's pretty hard to get with other varieties. Trust me on this one – once you've had a taste of pasta made from these gems, there's no going back. Brands like Napoli Antimo Caputo have seriously set the bar high when it comes to top-notch Italian flours; they're worth every dime.

- **The Rustic Touch of Semolina:** his is essentially the heart and soul of many old-school Italian pastas. Produced from coarsely milled durum wheat flour, semolina adds an earthy touch and robust texture to your meals. But wait - there's more! Semolina is particularly useful for making extruded types of pasta such as penne because its rich protein content helps maintain shape after being pushed through the die (extrusion process), ensuring those penne remains tubular perfection itself! So if you're trying out shapes that need form stability? You've got yourself a match in semolina!
- **The All-Purpose Alternative:** If you're just getting started or don't have specialized flours at hand, all-purpose flour can come to your rescue. While it may not offer the same level of refinement as "00" or semolina, it's a versatile option. For better results, you can even mix it with a bit of semolina or "00" flour to improve the texture and flavor.
- **What to Avoid:** Cake or pastry flours are a big no-no. Their low protein and gluten content will leave you with a pasta that's far from ideal. Similarly, strong bread flour can make your pasta too dense and chewy, making it more suitable for bread than pasta.

The gluten developed from the protein in your flour should offer both elasticity and plasticity. Elasticity allows the dough to stretch without tearing, essential for when you're rolling and shaping your pasta. Plasticity helps the dough hold its shape, crucial for intricate shapes like farfalle or fusilli.

So, choosing the right flour is not just a matter of preference; it's a science and an art. Your choice lays the foundation for everything that follows in your pasta-making journey. Choose wisely, and you'll be rewarded with pasta that's nothing short of perfection.

Importance of Egg Quality

So, you think an egg is just another ingredient in your pasta recipe? Think again! That little sphere of goodness holds everything together – it's the heart and soul of your pasta. Here's why you should care about its quality.

The Color of the Yolk: the yolk color spills some serious tea about an egg's quality. A deep golden yoke usually screams 'high-quality' - that chicken was probably well-fed and raised in good conditions! This rich-in-color-and-flavor yolk adds a pop to your pasta that those pale yolks can't even dream of achieving. Remember, we eat with our eyes first, and a pasta with a rich, golden hue is always more appetizing.

The Freshness Factor: there's nothing like fresh eggs when making dough for pasta. They have this tight structure giving us firmer, more elastic dough - exactly what we need for rolling and shaping our homemade noodles just right! A fresh egg delivers that perfect al dente texture – firm yet tender bite every time. Pro tip: check out the sell-by date or better yet grab them from a local farmer's market if possible– trust me on this one; You'll taste the difference!

Free-Range vs. Battery-Caged: Free-range eggs aren't just a kinder choice for the chickens - they're also better for you. Chickens that can stretch their legs tend to lay eggs packed with omega-3 fatty acids and Vitamin D. These goodies not only up the health factor in your pasta but also bring an extra touch of deliciousness that battery-caged egg-laid pasta simply can't compete with. So if it's within reach, make free-range your go-to.

Organic and Nutrient-Enriched Options: in recent years, the market has seen an influx of organic and nutrient-enriched eggs. These eggs come from chickens that have been fed a special diet, often rich in flaxseed, to boost the egg's nutrient content. The result is an eggy goodness with elevated nutrients levels which add another layer of flavor depth to any dish, especially our favorite: Pasta! Yes, they might be a little more expensive than regular ones - but think about it this way: no antibiotics or hormones mean cleaner fuel for your body.

Other optional ingredients

Ready to take your pasta game up a notch with some bonus ingredients? They're gonna add an explosion of flavor, a visual treat or even that unexpected twist. And the best part? You've got all the freedom in the world to experiment!

Vegetables: I'm talking beets, winter squash, garlic, peppers and carrots. Picture just how vibrant and flavorful your pasta will turn out!

Dried Herbs and Spices: if you're one who loves kickin' it up a notch on flavors, dried herbs and spices are about to become your new best friends! Try adding cayenne or smoked paprika when you make roasted red pepper pasta next time – trust me, the variety here is endless! Whether bold or subtle flavours rock your boat, you can control them.

Leafy Greens: don't overlook the leafy greens! Spinach, beet greens and kale, can add interesting flavors and colors to your pasta. Just remember to boil them for a few minutes, strain them very well (ideally squeeze out the excess water) and then puree. The result? A pasta that not only tastes great but also packs a nutritional punch.

When tinkering around with these optional extras, it's kinda important getting liquid-flour ratio perfect. For instance; adding veggie puree might mean cutting down little bit egg/water maintain sweet spot consistency. Or maybe add extra flour. Don't sweat though, I'll walk through specifics shortly.

THE PERFECT DOUGH RATIO

Crafting pasta isn't just about tossing some flour and eggs into a bowl; it's more like mastering the art of balance and moisture. Nail this, and your pasta will be the talk of circles far beyond your block. Screw up? Well, we don't want to venture down that road.

Egg to flour ratio

The general rule of thumb for making pasta is to use one medium egg and 100 grams of flour per person. Sounds simple enough, right? But ah, life is never that straightforward, especially in the kitchen!

Let's face it: Eggs can be trickier than they seem, sorta like snowflakes, never identical twins. They differ in size and weight which can play around with your dough hydration levels. You may therefore need to add flour if the dough is too sticky, or water if it is too stiff.

Now, let's pause for a moment to consider a more precise approach. To sidestep the variable of egg size, weighing your eggs is a viable solution. However, it's crucial to understand that the ideal hydration of homemade pasta (essentially the ratio of flour to liquid9 generally ranges between 45% and 50%, contingent on the type of pasta being made. When utilizing only eggs as the liquid component of the dough, the hydration calculation becomes a bit more complex. This is due to the fact that only 75% of the egg's weight accounts for the liquid part of the dough. For a simpler calculation, retaining a reference of 57g of egg for every 100g of flour, or 57%, might come in handy, although this isn't within the traditional hydration range.

Let's say you're cooking for two and you weigh your eggs to find they total 110 grams. To find out how much flour you'll need, you'd divide 110 by 0.57, which gives you about 193 grams of flour. Voilà! You've got a dough with the right hydration level, no matter the size of your eggs.

"But will this give me the same dough every time?" you might ask. Ah, if only it were that simple! You see, different flours have different water-absorbing capacities. Plus, the humidity in the air and the temperature in your kitchen can also affect your dough's hydration. And let's not forget, if you're adding special ingredients like vegetables, you'll have to account for their moisture content as well.

So, what's the solution? Well, my dears, as with many things in life, practice makes perfect. Over time, you'll develop a keen sense for when your dough needs a little more flour or a drop more water. You'll be able to adjust on the fly, making each pasta dish a unique masterpiece.

Adjusting ratios for different flours

Not all flours are created equal. Each type has its own unique characteristics, and understanding these can make all the difference in your pasta-making journey.

Firstly, let's talk about protein content. Flours with higher protein content, like bread flour, are more absorbent. They'll soak up more water, leading to a firmer dough. On the other hand, flours with lower protein content, like pastry or cake flour, will absorb less water, resulting in a softer, more delicate dough. So, if you're using a high-protein flour, you might need to add a bit more water to achieve that perfect hydration level we talked about earlier.

Moving onto another key player: The milling process. Finely milled flours have a larger surface area, allowing them to absorb more water. Coarser flours, like whole grain or semolina, will absorb less. So, if you're using a finely milled flour, be prepared to adjust your hydration levels accordingly.

Ah, and don't forget about the age of the flour! Yes, you heard me right. Freshly milled flour will absorb water differently than flour that's been sitting on the shelf for a while. As flour ages, it loses moisture, which can affect its water-absorbing capacity. So, always check the expiration date and try to use fresher flour when possible.

How do I adjust the ratios when using different flours? Well the answer lies in observation and adjustment. Start with the basic 57% hydration ratio we discussed earlier. As you mix your dough, pay close attention to its texture. If it feels too dry, add a bit more water, a teaspoon at a time. If it's too sticky, sprinkle in some more flour.

Remember, pasta-making is as much about feeling as it is about precise measurements. Your hands are the best tools you have. They'll tell you when the dough is just right. Over time, you'll develop a sixth sense for it, knowing exactly how to adjust your ratios for different flours.

Other ingredients ratio

The beauty of homemade pasta is that you can experiment with various ingredients to create something truly unique. But, of course, adding extra ingredients means we'll need to adjust our dough ratios a bit. Don't worry, I'll guide you through it, and we'll even explore some delightful recipes later on.

Let's start by talking about veggies. Adding pureed spinach, beetroot, or even carrots can give your pasta a vibrant hue and a subtle, earthy flavor. But remember, these vegetables contain water, which will affect your dough's hydration. So, you'll need to reduce the amount of egg or water you use. For example, if you're adding 50 grams of spinach puree, you might need to reduce the egg weight by about 30 grams to maintain that ideal hydration level.

Herbs are another great way to add flavor without drastically changing our liquid components - basil, parsley or rosemary would work wonderfully here! Just finely chop them down before mixing everything together for maximum aroma boost (and minimum effort!).

Moving on to spices now. Got some saffron lying around the kitchen? Maybe some paprika or turmeric? Toss a bit into your mix; they're gonna add an awesome dash of color and kickass flavor. The best part is these dry spices won't mess with how much moisture is in your dough – unless we're dealing with liquid forms like saffron water, then you gotta tweak those liquids just right.

For those looking to add some rich flavor, consider grating Parmesan or Pecorino cheese into the mix - however, be aware that this will make the dough heavier and so you may need to add more water for balance.

For something even bolder, why not try cocoa powder or squid ink? Cocoa is great in dessert pastas while squid ink gives seafood dishes an eye-catching jet-black hue. Just remember that a little goes a long way when it comes to these powerful ingredients! Just remember to adjust your hydration levels if you're using a liquid form of these ingredients.

Now, you might be thinking, "This sounds complicated!" But fear not, my dears. I will provide you with step-by-step recipes to help you create some of these special doughs. Each recipe will guide you through the process, making it easy to adjust your dough to perfection.

Think of creating delicious homemade pastas as like putting together a vibrant tapestry; each individual ingredient adds something special until everything comes alive in harmony. Don't worry if things don't turn out perfect at first – a bit of practice and a dash of intuition makes perfect after all!

Special note on weighing ingredients

Let's not forget what we've discussed before: pasta-making is as much about feeling as it is about precise measurements. You might be wondering, "Why the emphasis on weighing then?" Well, let's take a moment to consider this.

Regarding flour, for example, when you measure with a cup, the weight can vary significantly. A cup of flour can weigh anywhere from 120 to 150 grams, depending on how you fill the cup. That's a 30-gram difference, my dears, and in the world of pasta-making, that's enough to turn your perfect fettuccine into a sticky mess or a crumbly disaster.

On weighing eggs, on the other hand, we have discussed this before, understanding how helpful it can be to know exactly the amount in grams of eggs we need.

You see, there are countless variables that can affect the final outcome of your pasta dough. The humidity in the air, the temperature of your kitchen, and even the quality of your ingredients can all play a role. Weighing your ingredients helps to control the major variables that have a significant impact on your dough's consistency, such as the flour and eggs. By doing so, you're setting a strong foundation for your pasta dough, one that's less susceptible to the whims of these external factors.

Now, once you've got that foundation, that's where your senses and experience come into play. The feel of the dough between your fingers, the way it responds when you knead it, these are things that a scale can't measure. And as you become more experienced, you'll find that you can make minor adjustments on the fly, adding a sprinkle of flour here or a dash of water there, to get the texture just right.

So, in essence, weighing your ingredients isn't about eliminating the need for sensory input or experience. Quite the opposite! It's about limiting the major variables so that you can focus on fine-tuning the minor ones. It's about giving you more control over the process, so that you can let your creativity shine without worrying about the basics. Think of it like this: a musician needs to know the basic scales before they can improvise a soul-stirring solo. Similarly, by weighing your ingredients, you're learning the basic "scales" of pasta-making, setting the stage for you to "improvise" with confidence and flair.

And here's a little tip that even my Nonna passed down to me: always weigh your container first and zero out the scale, what we Italians call "fare la tara." This ensures that you're only weighing the ingredients and not the container. It's a small step, but it makes a world of difference, especially when you're dealing with precise measurements.

So while the scale is your ally in achieving consistency, your senses are your guides in achieving artistry. Together, they make a formidable team that can tackle any pasta-making challenge that comes your way.

THE ART OF MIXING AND KNEADING

Mixing and kneading dough is basically the heart of pasta-making, right? In this part, we're going to dive deep into how you can turn basic ingredients into a magical lump of potential. We'll compare the time-honored traditional well method with the modern convenience of a food processor. Plus, I'm gonna let you in on some secrets for knowing when your dough has hit that sweet spot and share tricks for getting it just the right texture.

The Two Method For Mixing

Now, let's talk about the two main ways to mix and knead your pasta dough: the traditional well method and the food processor method.

The traditional Well Method

The well method is as old as Nonna's secret recipes. Picture this: a mound of flour on a wooden board, a well in the center, and eggs carefully cracked into it. With a fork, you gently whisk the eggs, gradually incorporating the flour from the edges. It's a tactile experience, one where you feel every grain of flour merging with the eggs. The process is slow, deliberate, and incredibly satisfying. You knead the dough with your hands, feeling the gluten develop under your touch.

Pros:

- Tactile experience allows for better control over the dough.
- No special equipment needed.
- The slow process allows for better gluten development.

Cons:

- Time-consuming.
- Can be messy.
- Requires some skill and experience.

The Stand Mixer Method

In today's fast-paced world, the stand mixer has become a staple in many kitchens, offering a blend of tradition and modernity. This method is a middle-ground between the old-world charm of hand-kneading and the rapid efficiency of food processors. With a stand mixer, you can attach a dough hook, add your ingredients, and let the machine do the work. It's a hands-free approach that still allows for some level of control and customization. You can adjust the speed, pause to check the dough's texture, and even finish off with a bit of hand-kneading if you like

Pros:

- Quick and efficient, great for those short on time.
- Less physically demanding.
- Consistent mixing due to machine precision.

Cons:

- Less tactile experience; you won't "feel" the dough as much.
- Requires owning a stand mixer, which can be expensive.

So, which method should you choose? If you're new to pasta-making, starting with the well method can give you a deeper understanding of how dough behaves. It's like learning to drive stick before going automatic. However, if you're pressed for time or not keen on the hands-on experience, the stand mixer method is a perfectly acceptable alternative.

In conclusion, both methods have their merits. The traditional well method offers a sensory experience that's deeply rooted in tradition, while the stand mixer brings modern convenience to the table. The choice, my dear friends, is yours to make.

How to Mix Ingredients

Mixing ingredients might seem like a straightforward task, but when it comes to pasta-making, the devil is in the details. The way you mix your ingredients can significantly affect the texture and quality of your final product. In this section, we'll delve into the step-by-step guide on how to properly mix your ingredients and share some invaluable tips to ensure you get it right every time.

Step-by-step guide:

1. Prepare Your Workspace:

Before you begin, ensure you have a clean, flat surface. A wooden board or a clean countertop works best. Sprinkle a bit of flour on the surface to prevent the dough from sticking.

2. Measure Your Ingredients:

Always start by measuring out your ingredients. This ensures consistency and helps you get the best results every time. Remember, precision is key, especially when you're just starting out.

3. Creating the Flour Well:

Pour your flour onto your workspace, shaping it into a mound. Using your fingers or the back of a spoon, create a well in the center, deep enough to hold the eggs and any other wet ingredients. If you prefer a tidier approach, you can opt for mixing your ingredients in a large bowl. This method is particularly useful for those who don't want flour scattered all over their kitchen.

4. Add the Eggs (and other wet ingredients if used):

Crack the eggs into the well. If you're using other wet ingredients, like vegetable purées for colored pasta, add them in now.

5. Gradually Mix:

Using a fork, gently whisk the eggs, slowly incorporating the flour from the edges of the well. Continue this motion, drawing more and more flour into the mix. As the mixture starts coming together, you can use your hands to gently fold in the remaining flour.

6. Combine Until a Dough Forms:

Once most of the flour is incorporated and the mixture has a shaggy, dough-like consistency, it's time to bring it all together. Use your hands to fold and press the dough, ensuring all the flour is absorbed.

7.Check the Consistency:

The dough should be firm but not too dry. If it's too sticky, add a sprinkle of flour. If it's too dry and crumbly, you can add a few drops of water or another egg yolk.

8.Last tip:

Before kneading, let the dough rest (covered with a bowl) for about 10 minutes, this will make kneading much easier, believe me.

For those who have a stand mixer, this appliance can make the mixing process even easier. Attach the dough hook and add your flour and eggs into the mixer bowl. Start the mixer on a low speed to combine the ingredients. Once the dough starts to form, increase the speed to medium for about 5-7 minutes until the dough is smooth and elastic. Keep an eye on the texture; you may need to add a bit more flour or water to get the right consistency. Using this method, the kneading step will not be necessary. Once the 5-7 minutes are over, cover the dough to prevent it from drying out and wait 5-10 minutes. Next form a ball with the dough, cover it tightly with plastic wrap and let it rest for 30 minutes before proceeding with the rolling stage.

The Art of Kneading

This is where your dough transforms from a shaggy mass into a smooth, elastic ball, ready to be rolled and shaped into your favorite pasta. Kneading is more than just a mechanical process; it's a labor of love that develops the gluten in the flour, giving your pasta its structure and bite. Let's delve into the intricacies of this essential step.

1. Initial Pressing:

Start by pressing the dough together with your hands to form a cohesive ball.

2. Push and Fold:

Place the dough on a clean, floured surface. Use the heel of your hand to push the dough away from you, then fold it back over itself.

3. Quarter Turn:

Give the dough a quarter turn, and then push and fold again. This action helps to align the gluten strands in the dough, which is crucial for elasticity.

4. Repeat:

Continue this push, fold, and turn process for about 8-10 minutes. You'll notice the dough becoming smoother and more elastic as you go.

5. Resting Time:

If you notice that the dough does not become smooth and soft but tends to tear and be hard, do not continue kneading; you will make it worse. The dough is telling you that it needs to rest and relax. So stop for 5-10 minutes by covering the dough with a bowl and then resume. This short break allows the gluten to relax, making the dough easier to work with when you return. You can safely repeat this step more than once if necessary.

6. Final Shaping:

Once you're satisfied with the dough's texture, shape it into a ball and let it rest covered tightly with plastic wrap for at least 30 minutes before rolling it out. This resting period allows the gluten to relax and the moisture to distribute evenly, resulting in a more uniform texture.

Tips for a perfect dough

But how do you know when your dough has been kneaded to perfection? Well, there are several telltale signs that can guide you, and with experience, you'll develop an intuitive sense for it. Here are some indicators to look for:

- **Smooth Surface:** Initially, your dough will have a rough, shaggy appearance. As you knead, it should transform into a smooth, elastic ball. If your dough has a smooth surface and a slight sheen, you're on the right track.
- **Springiness:** Press your finger lightly into the dough. If it springs back quickly, that's a good sign that the gluten has developed sufficiently.
- **Windowpane Test:** This is a classic baker's test. Take a small piece of dough and gently stretch it between your fingers. If it forms a thin, translucent membrane without tearing, your dough is ready.
- **Consistency:** The dough should feel pliable but not sticky. If it sticks to your fingers or the work surface, it might need a bit more flour. Conversely, if it feels too dry and crumbly, a few drops of water can help.
- **Cohesion:** The dough should hold together well and not fall apart when you're rolling or shaping it. This is a sign that the gluten strands have aligned and are providing structure to your dough.
- **Intuition:** Sometimes, it's just a gut feeling. The dough will feel 'right' under your hands, and you'll know it's ready for the next stage.

Step-by-Step Recipe Dough

In this enlightening section, we'll walk through various recipes that cater to different needs and tastes. From the classic egg pasta dough that's been passed down through generations to innovative vegan and gluten-free options, we've got something for everyone. We'll even explore the vibrant world of colored pasta doughs and the aromatic realm of spice-infused pasta. For the mixing and kneading stages, you can refer back to the previous sections where we've covered all the tips and tricks to achieve the perfect texture. While the general principles remain the same, some recipes in this section will include specific Directions. for mixing, as there may be slight variations depending on the ingredients used. So, roll up those sleeves and clear some counter space; it's time to make some pasta magic happen!

Classic Egg Pasta Dough

The classic egg pasta dough is the undisputed champ of Italian pasta creation. It's this very dough that grandmas and seasoned chefs around the world can't live without, forming a launchpad for most of those iconic shapes and dishes we know and love. The recipe? Simplicity itself - just high-quality flour and fresh eggs. What you get is a versatile piece of culinary magic that easily morphs into anything from fettuccine to your favorite ravioli.

SERVING: 4-6 people

INGREDIENTS:

- 400 g "Tipo 00" Flour or all-purpose flour
- 228 g Eggs – about four medium eggs

Semolina Pasta Dough

When it comes to leveling up your pasta game, semolina flour should be at the top of your grocery list. This golden-hued grain gives your pasta some serious texture along with an irresistible 'al dente' crunchiness every bite deserves . Not only does semolina bring strength to the structure but also ensures each shape stands tall on its own! So whether you're loyal to our old friend 'Tipo 00', or itching for something new in the kitchen, introducing semolina into your mix could spell out a whole universe worth exploring in pasta land.

SERVING: 4 -6 people

INGREDIENTS:

- 200g "Tipo 00" Flour or all-purpose flour
- 200g Semolina Flour
- 228g Eggs – about four medium eggs

Vegan Pasta Dough

The Vegan Pasta Dough recipe is a versatile base that can be used to create a variety of pasta types, from spaghetti to ravioli and fettuccine. This eggless recipe is perfect for those who follow a vegan diet but still want to enjoy the art of pasta-making.

SERVING: 4-6 people

INGREDIENTS:

- 150 g "Tipo 00" Flour or all-purpose flour
- 150 g semolina flour or sub more regular flour
- ½ tsp salt
- 150 ml water (room temperature)
- 2 tsp olive oil

DIRECTIONS:

1. Combine the flour and salt in a large mixing bowl, forming a well in the middle.
2. Add the olive oil into the well.
3. Slowly add water to the well, a little at a time, mixing continuously to incorporate the wet and dry ingredients. If the dough feels too sticky, add a bit more flour; if it's too dry, add a small amount of additional water.

Gluten-Free Pasta Dough

For those who are gluten-sensitive or simply prefer a gluten-free option, this recipe is a game-changer. You won't feel like you're missing out on the authentic pasta experience. This gluten-free dough is versatile, allowing you to make virtually any kind of pasta. The recipe involves a few more ingredients than the traditional one, but the end result is well worth it.

SERVING: 4-6 people

INGREDIENTS:

- 280 g all-purpose gluten-free flour blend
- 1 teaspoon xanthan gum (don't add if your blend already contains it)
- 45 g tapioca starch/flour
- ½ teaspoon kosher salt
- 100 g eggs at room temperature, beaten (weighed out of shell)

- 50 g egg yolks at room temperature, beaten
- 14 g extra virgin olive oil
- 80 g warm water

DIRECTIONS:

1. In a large bowl, blend the dry components. Next, incorporate the olive oil, beaten eggs, and egg yolks. Stir until well combined.
2. Gradually introduce the warm water while stirring. Continue to mix until the dough is well-formed. If the dough feels too rigid, add a little more water to make it more flexible.

Colored Pasta Dough

As promised here are some colorful pasta recipes. These are some of the possible special recipes that I hope you can use to unleash your creativity and create new combinations.

Black squid ink pasta

SERVING: 4-6 people

INGREDIENTS:

- 280g "Tipo 00" Flour or all-purpose flour
- 2 whole large eggs (114g)
- 4 yolks from 4 large eggs (72g)

·4 teaspoons squid ink (about 17g)

DIRECTIONS:

1. On a large, clean work surface or in a large bowl, pour flour into a mound. Create a well in the center that's about 4 inches wide.
2. Add the whole eggs, egg yolks, and squid ink into the well. Using a fork, beat the ingredients thoroughly to combine.
3. Gradually incorporate the flour into the wet mixture until a wet, sticky dough forms.
4. Begin to fold additional flour into the dough, turning it roughly 45 degrees each time, until the dough feels firm and dry, forming a craggy-looking ball. This should take about 2 to 5 minutes.

Orange tomato pasta

SERVING: 4-6 people

INGREDIENTS:

- 280 gr "Tipo 00" Flour or all-purpose flour
- 5 yolks from 5 large eggs (90 gr)
- 1 whole large egg (57gr)
- 56 gr tomato paste

DIRECTIONS:

1. On a large, clean work surface or in a large bowl, pour the flour into a mound. Create a well in the center that's about 4 inches wide.

2. Add the whole egg, egg yolks, and tomato paste into the well. Using a fork, beat the ingredients thoroughly to combine.

3. Gradually incorporate the flour into the wet mixture, stirring until a wet, sticky dough forms.

4. Begin to fold additional flour into the dough, turning it roughly 45 degrees each time, until the dough feels firm and dry, forming a craggy-looking ball. This should take about 2 to 5 minutes.

Green spinach pasta

SERVING: 4-6 people

INGREDIENTS:

For the dough:

- 280 gr "Tipo 00" Flour or all-purpose flour
- 5 yolks from 5 large eggs (90 gr)
- 1 whole large egg (57gr)
- 56gr spinach purée

For the spinach purée:

- 1 bunch fresh spinach (about 280 gr), rinsed and stems trimmed

DIRECTIONS:

1. Bring a large pot of water to a boil. In the meantime, prepare a large bowl filled with cold water and ice. Add the rinsed and trimmed spinach to the boiling water and cook for 15-30 seconds. Drain the spinach and immediately plunge it into the bowl of ice-cold water. Once cooled, drain again (using a salad spinner) and use a hand blender or food processor to purée the spinach until smooth.

2. On a large, clean work surface or in a large bowl, pour the flour into a mound. Create a well in the center, about 4 inches wide.

3. Pour the whole egg, egg yolks, and spinach purée into the well. Using a fork, beat the ingredients thoroughly to combine.

4. Gradually incorporate the flour into the wet ingredients, mixing until a wet, sticky dough forms.

5. Begin to fold additional flour into the dough, turning it roughly 45 degrees each time, until the dough feels firm and dry, forming a craggy-looking ball. This should take about 2 to 5 minutes.

Purple-red beet pasta

SERVING: 4-6 people

INGREDIENTS:

For the dough:

- 280 gr "Tipo 00" Flour or all-purpose flour,
- 5 yolks from 5 large eggs (90 gr)
- 1 whole large egg (57gr)
- 56gr beet purée

For the beet purée:

- 2 small beets (about 200 gr), rinsed and trimmed

DIRECTIONS:

1. Heat a pot of water until it reaches a boiling point. Place the cleaned and cut beets into the boiling water and cook them until a fork can easily go through them, which should take around 40-45 minutes. After that, drain the water and allow the beets to cool down. Once cooled, remove the skin and blend them into a smooth purée using either a hand blender or a food processor.

2. On a large, clean work surface or in a large bowl, pour the flour into a mound. Create a well in the center, about 4 inches wide.

3. Pour the whole egg, egg yolks, and beet purée. Using a fork, beat the ingredients thoroughly to combine.

4. Gradually incorporate the flour into the wet ingredients, mixing until a wet, sticky dough forms.

5. Begin to fold additional flour into the dough, turning it roughly 45 degrees each time, until the dough feels firm and dry, forming a craggy-looking ball. This should take about 2 to 5 minutes.

THE CRAFT OF ROLLING AND SHAPING

THE ROLLING STAGE

Rolling is that game-changing moment in pasta-making where your diligently kneaded dough morphs into gorgeous, light sheets, ready to be shaped as you wish. Think of it as the dough's debutante ball, where it gets to show off its texture, elasticity, and potential. This stage is not just about flattening; it's about refining. It's where you start to see the fruits of your labor and where the dough's texture and elasticity truly come into play.

The rolling phase holds critical significance for a couple of reasons. Firstly, it affects the pasta's final texture - an expertly rolled out dough cooks uniformly and traps sauces more efficiently adding depth to every bite. Secondly, it gears up the dough for shaping – whether you're making fettuccine, ravioli or any other form a consistently rolled-out piece is easier to manage guaranteeing uniformity across each serving.

In essence, rolling is the bridge between your basic dough and the myriad pasta shapes you can create. It's a simple yet vital step, and mastering it will elevate your homemade pasta to a new level.

In this section, we'll walk you through the essentials: from prepping your dough to the actual rolling process, whether you're using a manual machine or a KitchenAid attachment. We'll also cover common issues and how to fix them. Ready to roll? Let's get started!

Preparation Before Rolling

Before you even think about feeding that dough through the rollers, there are some essential preparatory steps you need to take. These steps are often overlooked but are crucial for achieving that perfect, silky-smooth pasta sheet. Let's break down the preparation process so that you're fully equipped for the rolling stage.

- **Divide and Conquer**

First things first, you don't want to work with your entire dough ball at once. It's much easier to manage smaller portions. So, divide your dough into manageable pieces, usually about the size of a lemon or a small apple. This makes it easier to feed the dough through the rollers and ensures that you get an even thickness throughout. Plus, smaller pieces are less likely to dry out as you work. Important note: keep the portions you're not currently using covered with plastic wrap to prevent them from drying out.

- **Lightly Flour, But Be Cautious**

Lightly flour the surface of your dough portions. This prevents sticking and helps the dough glide smoothly through the rollers. Instead of using regular flour, opt for semolina. Semolina is less absorbent than regular flour, which means it won't significantly alter the texture of your dough. Lightly dust both the dough and the rollers with semolina to prevent sticking. This will ensure a smooth rolling process without compromising the dough's quality.

- **Pre-Shape Your Dough**

It's a good idea to pre-shape your dough into a rough oval shape. This makes it easier to feed through the rollers and results in a more uniform sheet. You can use your hands or a rolling pin for this initial shaping. The key is to get it into a form that will fit comfortably within the width of your pasta machine's rollers.

- **Check Your Rollers**

Make sure your pasta machine's rollers are clean and free from any old dough or flour. Any leftover particles can imprint on your fresh dough and affect the final texture. A quick wipe with a dry cloth is usually sufficient to clean the rollers.

- **Set Up Your Workspace**

Last but not least, set up your workspace for efficiency. Place your pasta machine on a stable surface and ensure you have enough room to work. Keep your divided, floured dough portions within arm's reach, along with extra flour for dusting. If you're using a manual machine, make sure it's clamped securely to the table to prevent any wobbling or shifting during rolling.

By taking the time to prepare, you're setting yourself up for success in the rolling stage. Each of these steps plays a vital role in ensuring that your dough rolls out smoothly, evenly, and without any hitches. So, don't rush through the preparation; give it the attention it deserves, and you'll be rewarded with pasta that's nothing short of perfection.

The Rolling Process

Alright, you've prepped your dough, your workspace is set up, and you're ready to roll, literally! So, let's get into the nitty-gritty of how to do it right. Trust me, a little know-how goes a long way in making your pasta-making journey a smooth one.

- **Starting Wide, Going Narrow**

Always start at the widest setting on your pasta machine. This is usually labeled as '0' or '1' depending on the brand.

Why start wide? Well, it's all about gradually stretching the gluten in the dough, making it more pliable and easier to work with. If you jump straight to a narrow setting, you risk tearing the dough or making it uneven. So, patience is key here.

- **The First Pass**

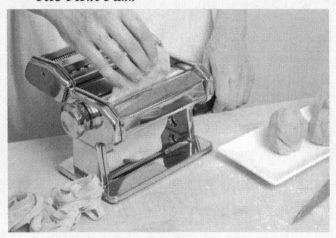

Take your pre-shaped, lightly floured oval of dough and feed it through the rollers while turning the crank (if you're using a manual machine) or setting the motor speed (if you're using a KitchenAid attachment). The speed at which you turn the crank can significantly impact the quality of your pasta. Turn it too fast, and you risk tearing the dough or making it uneven. Turn it too slowly, and you might end up with pasta that's too thick or doughy. The key is to find a moderate, steady pace. This allows the rollers to catch and stretch the dough evenly, resulting in a smooth, consistent sheet. For those using a KitchenAid attachment medium speed is generally recommended for most pasta types

- **Folding and Turning**

After the first pass, you'll notice that the dough is elongated but might look a bit rough around the edges. No worries, that's totally normal. Fold the dough in half or into thirds and pass it through the widest setting again. This process, known as laminating, helps to create a smooth, even texture. Do this a couple of times until the dough feels smooth to the touch.

- **Gradually Narrowing the Gap**

Once you're satisfied with the texture, it's time to narrow the roller setting. Move to the next setting and roll the dough through again. Continue this process, reducing the setting one notch at a time, until you reach your desired thickness. Don't worry too much about the exact thickness at this stage; in the following sections, we'll delve into the specifics of the ideal thickness for each type of pasta.

- **The Final Pass**

When you're at your final setting, give the dough one last pass to ensure it's perfectly even. By now, you should have a beautiful, smooth sheet of pasta that's ready for cutting or shaping. If you notice any imperfections, don't stress, homemade pasta is all about rustic charm, after all.

- **A Few More Tips**

1. If at any point the dough starts to stick, don't hesitate to sprinkle a little more semolina on both the dough and the rollers.
2. If you're using a KitchenAid attachment, the medium speed setting usually works well for most dough types.
3. If your dough sheet becomes too long to manage, simply cut it in half and work with smaller lengths.

And there you have it! You've successfully navigated the rolling stage, and you're one step closer to pasta perfection. Remember, practice makes perfect, so don't be too hard on yourself if things don't go smoothly the first time.

Troubleshooting Common Issues

The rolling stage, while exciting, can also be fraught with challenges that may leave you scratching your head. But don't worry; we've got you covered. Let's delve into some common issues you might encounter during the rolling stage and how to fix them.

- **Dough Has Irregular Hard Spots**

What Happened: You left the dough uncovered for too long, causing it to dry out in spots.

What to Do: Don't panic. Simply proceed with rolling it out using a rolling pin to smooth out those hard areas.

- **Dough Breaks on the Sides**

What Happened: The dough wasn't thin enough for the setting you chose on your pasta machine (those numbers on the side that regulate the dough's thickness).

What to Do: Dial back to a less thin setting on your machine and roll the dough through again.

- **Long Cut in the Middle or Side of the Dough**

What Happened: A small piece of dough got stuck in the machine, causing a tear in your sheet.

What to Do: Clean the machine with a brush to remove the offending piece. To prevent this in the future, always use fresh flour straight from the package when you need extra flour for kneading.

- **Dough Sticking to the Rollers**

What Happened: The dough is too wet, or the rollers are dirty.

What to Do: Lightly dust the dough with semolina to prevent sticking and ensure your rollers are clean.

- **Uneven Rolling**

What Happened: Inconsistent feeding or uneven pressure.

What to Do: Feed the dough evenly and maintain a steady speed, whether you're using a manual crank or a KitchenAid attachment.

- **Dough Becomes Too Elastic**

What Happened: Over-kneading has made the dough too elastic.

What to Do: Let the dough rest for a few minutes to relax the gluten, then proceed with rolling.

- **Dough Cracking or Breaking**

What Happened: The dough is too dry.

What to Do: Lightly spritz the dough with water and knead it until it reaches the right consistency.

- **Rollers Aren't Catching the Dough**

What Happened: The dough is too wet or slippery.

What to Do: A light dusting of flour can provide the necessary traction for the rollers to catch the dough.

THE SHAPE OF PASTA

Within the art of pasta-making, the shape is more than just aesthetics: it's about tradition, regionality, and the perfect pairing with sauces. In this section, we'll journey through Italy's iconic pasta shapes, understanding their unique characteristics and regional ties. But it doesn't stop at exploration. We'll also guide you step-by-step, ensuring that you not only appreciate the beauty of each shape but also master the techniques to create them. From the classic spaghetti to the intricate ravioli, get ready to immerse yourself in a world where pasta is both history and craft.

Step-by-Step Guide

Now that we've rolled our dough to perfection, we're on the cusp of something truly magical. It's the last step before we transform our dough into the pasta shapes we love. This is the moment to fine-tune the thickness of your dough one last time.

We'll guide you through the settings for the two most popular models, the Mercato Atlas 150 and the KitchenAid pasta roller/cutter set, to ensure you achieve the ideal thickness for your chosen pasta shape. Then, it's time to engage the right attachment and cut that dough into culinary works of art!

So, gather around as we delve into the specifics of making various pasta shapes, from spaghetti to fettuccine, tagliatelle, and more. Trust me, it's easier than you think, and oh-so-rewarding.

- **Spaghetti**

  <u>Accessory Needed:</u> Spaghetti cutter attachment

  <u>Approximate Thickness:</u> 2mm

  DIRECTIONS:

  a. Set your pasta maker to setting 4 or 5 if you're using a Mercato Atlas, or to setting 3 or 4 if you're using a KitchenAid attachment.

  b. Roll the dough through the machine a couple of times to achieve the desired thickness.

  c. Once you've rolled out your dough, place the pasta sheet on a flat and floured surface, this could be a baking tray or a countertop. Then sprinkle with flour and leave to dry for 10-15 minutes (This ensures that the dough is firm enough to be properly cut).

  d. Attach the spaghetti cutter attachment to your pasta maker, ensuring that the pasta sheets are of adequate width to pass through the attachment.

  e. Prepare your pasta sheets to be approximately 20-25cm long; you can either pre-cut them to this length or trim the noodles later.

  f. Feed the pasta sheets through the spaghetti attachment while turning the crank (or operating the KitchenAid motor).

  g. As the spaghetti emerges, collect it in a large bowl containing a handful of flour.

  h. Gently toss the spaghetti in the flour to prevent the strands from sticking together.

  i. Lay the finished spaghetti on a dry tea towel while you process the remaining dough.

- **Tagliatelle**

  Accessory Needed: Pasta Cutter/Sharp Knife

  Approximate Thickness: 1mm

  DIRECTIONS:

  a. Set your pasta maker to setting 6 or 7 if you're using a Mercato Atlas 150, or to setting 5 or 6 if you're using a KitchenAid attachment.

  b. Roll the dough through the machine a couple of times to achieve the desired thickness.

  c. Once you've rolled out your dough, place the pasta sheet on a flat and floured surface, this could be a baking tray or a countertop. Then sprinkle with flour and leave to dry for 10-15 minutes (This ensures that the dough is firm enough to be properly cut).

  d. Prepare your pasta sheets to be approximately 20-25cm long; either pre-cut them to this length or trim the noodles later.

  e. How to Cut:
     - Pasta Cutter: Utilize either a straight or serrated pasta cutter to cut the dough sheets into ribbons approximately 8mm wide. For straight lines and uniformity, you may use a ruler if you wish.
     - Sharp Knife: Begin by folding the dough sheets from the shorter sides to form a loose log. Using a sharp knife, cut this dough roll into strands around 8mm in width. After cutting, promptly unfurl each strand of tagliatelle and sprinkle with some extra flour to prevent sticking, if needed.

  f. Collect the cut tagliatelle in a large bowl containing a handful of flour.

  g. Gently toss the tagliatelle in the flour to prevent the strands from sticking together.

  h. Lay the finished tagliatelle on a dry tea towel while you process the remaining dough.

- **Fettuccine**

  Accessory Needed: Fettuccine Cutter Attachment

  Approximate Thickness: 1mm to 1.5mm

  DIRECTIONS:

  a. Set your pasta maker to setting 6 or 7 if you're using a Mercato Atlas 150, or to setting 5 or 6 if you're using a KitchenAid attachment.

  b. Roll the dough through the machine a couple of times to achieve the desired thickness.

  c. Once you've rolled out your dough, place the pasta sheet on a flat and floured surface, this could be a baking tray or a countertop. Then sprinkle with flour and leave to dry for 10-15 minutes (This ensures that the dough is firm enough to be properly cut).

  d. Attach the fettuccine cutter attachment to your pasta maker, ensuring that the pasta sheets are of adequate width to pass through the attachment.

  e. Prepare your pasta sheets to be approximately 20-25cm long; either pre-cut them to this length or trim the noodles later.

  f. Feed the pasta sheets through the fettuccine attachment while turning the crank or operating the KitchenAid motor.

g. As the fettuccine emerges, collect it in a large bowl containing a handful of flour.

h. Gently toss the fettuccine in the flour to prevent the strands from sticking together.

i. Lay the finished fettuccine on a dry tea towel while you process the remaining dough.

If you want to cut them by hand, the process is the same as for tagliatelle, however, the width should be of 6,5mm

- ## Pappardelle

  Accessory Needed: Pasta Cutter/Sharp Knife

  Approximate Thickness: 1mm

  DIRECTIONS:

  a. Set your pasta maker to setting 6 or 7 if you're using a Mercato Atlas 150, or to setting 5 or 6 if you're using a KitchenAid attachment.

  b. Roll the dough through the machine a couple of times to achieve the desired thickness.

  c. Once you've rolled out your dough, place the pasta sheet on a flat and floured surface, this could be a baking tray or a countertop. Then sprinkle with flour and leave to dry for 10-15 minutes (This ensures that the dough is firm enough to be properly cut).

  d. Prepare your pasta sheets to be approximately 20-25cm long; either pre-cut them to this length or trim the noodles later.

  e. How to Cut:
     - Follow the same cutting procedure as for Tagliatelle, but ensure that the width of the pappardelle is between 2.5cm and 3cm.

  f. Collect the cut pappardelle in a large bowl containing a handful of flour.

  g. Gently toss the pappardelle in the flour to prevent the strands from sticking together.

  h. Lay the finished pappardelle on a dry tea towel while you process the remaining dough.

- ## Lasagna Noodles

  Accessory Needed: Standard Roller Attachment

  Approximate Thickness: 1mm

  DIRECTIONS:

  a. Set your pasta maker to setting 6 if you're using a Mercato Atlas 150, or to setting 4 or 5 if you're using a KitchenAid attachment.

  b. Roll the dough through the machine a couple of times to achieve the desired thickness.

  c. Cut the pasta sheets to fit the dimensions of the baking dish you'll be using to assemble the lasagna.

  d. Lay the lasagna noodles, obtained from the first ball of dough, in a single layer on a baking sheet lined with parchment paper. Cover with another sheet of parchment paper to prevent them from drying out.

  e. Repeat the process with the remaining three pieces of dough.

  f. Stack the noodles made from each of the four pieces of dough in the baking dish, placing a sheet of parchment paper between each layer to prevent sticking.

- **Ravioli**

  Accessory Needed: Pasta Cutter

  Approximate Thickness: 1mm

  DIRECTIONS:

  a. Set your pasta maker to setting 6 or 7 if you're using a Mercato Atlas 150, or to setting 4 or 5 if you're using a KitchenAid attachment.

  b. Roll the dough through the machine a couple of times to achieve the desired thickness.

  c. Once done, gently trim the rounded edges. Cut the dough into sheets that are 10-12 inches long. The sheets don't have to be perfect; you'll do additional trimming later. Place them on a baking sheet and cover with parchment paper. Continue this process with the remaining three pieces of dough.

  d. Take a single sheet of dough. If you're a beginner, I suggest placing your chosen filling (measured in round teaspoons) in the center of the sheet, spaced about two fingers apart. If your sheets are 10-12 inches long, you can place four teaspoons of filling. For those with more manual skill, instead of a single row of filling, create two parallel rows of four dollops each. This way, you can make eight ravioli from one sheet, reducing dough waste.

  e. Using a slightly damp pastry brush, wet the dough around each mound of filling (do not overdo it only serves to make the two sheets of dough stick together). Place a second sheet of dough over the first, aligning it like a sandwich. Press the dough around each ravioli portion with dry, floured fingers to seal it, taking care not to trap air inside.

  f. Cut the ravioli into your preferred shape using your chosen tool, such as a straight-edged or fluted pasta wheel. Use your fingertips to ensure each pocket of dough is securely sealed along the edges.

  g. Transfer the finished ravioli to a baking sheet lined with parchment paper and sprinkled with semolina flour. Cover with a towel or another inverted baking sheet. Repeat these steps to assemble and cut the remaining ravioli.

Additional consideration:

You should know that there are myriad ways to craft ravioli, each with its own set of tools and accessories. From Ravioli Molds to Ravioli Stamps, and even specialized attachments for the KitchenAid (though I must say, I wouldn't particularly recommend that last one.) You see, the beauty of the hand-cut method I've shared with you is its simplicity. It doesn't require any special tools or additional purchases. All you need are your hands, a pasta cutter, and a little bit of that Italian love we all have inside us. This way, you can still create delicious, homemade ravioli without the fuss of extra gadgets.

- **Capellini**

  Accessory Needed: Capellini Cutter Attachment

  Approximate Thickness: 0.5mm to 0.6mm

  DIRECTIONS:

  a. Set your pasta maker to setting 8 or 9 if you're using a Mercato Atlas 150, or to setting 7 or 8 if you're using a KitchenAid attachment.

a. Roll the dough through the machine a couple of times to achieve the desired thickness.

b. Attach the capellini cutter attachment to your pasta maker, ensuring that the pasta sheets are of adequate width to pass through the attachment.

c. Prepare your pasta sheets to be approximately 20-25cm long; either pre-cut them to this length or trim the noodles later.

d. Feed the pasta sheets through the capellini attachment while turning the crank or operating the KitchenAid motor.

e. As the capellini emerges, collect it in a large bowl containing a handful of flour.

f. Gently toss the capellini in the flour to prevent the strands from sticking together.

g. Lay the finished capellini on a dry tea towel while you process the remaining dough.

I want to close this section regarding pasta shape with a thought: the thickness settings I've shared are born from my own experience and personal taste. They are not set in stone but rather a starting point for your own culinary adventures. The beauty of homemade pasta lies in its versatility and the freedom it offers for personalization.

Feel empowered to experiment with different thicknesses and shapes to suit your palate. After all, the best pasta is the one that you enjoy the most. So go ahead, roll that dough a little thicker or cut those fettuccine a bit narrower, it's your kitchen, your rules.

Here's to many delightful pasta-making sessions ahead, filled with creativity, joy, and of course, deliciousness!

THE FINAL STEP: COOKING OR STORAGE

After the meticulous process of selecting the right ingredients, kneading, rolling, and shaping, we've finally arrived at the grand finale: the decision to cook or store. This chapter is dedicated to guiding you through this crucial juncture. Whether you're eager to savor your freshly made pasta right away or you're planning to save it for a special occasion, we've got you covered. We'll delve into the nuances of cooking various pasta types to perfection and provide insights on preserving their freshness for later use. So, let's embark on this final leg of our pasta-making journey together!

THE COOKING PROCESS

Crafting the perfect dough is only half the journey. The real magic unfolds when we introduce our delicate creation to boiling water, transforming it from a raw masterpiece into a culinary delight.

Cooking fresh homemade pasta is a dance: a delicate balance of timing, temperature, and technique. It's not just about boiling water and tossing in the pasta. It's about understanding the unique nature of fresh pasta, being attentive to its needs, and ensuring it's cooked to perfection. After all, what's the point of putting in all that effort to make fresh pasta if we don't cook it with the same love and care?

In this section, we'll guide you through the nuances of cooking fresh pasta, ensuring that every strand or shape you've lovingly crafted reaches its full potential. We'll explore the art of achieving that coveted "al dente" texture, the importance of salting the water just right, and the little tricks that make a big difference.

Drying Pasta Before Cooking:

You might be wondering, "Why would I dry my freshly made pasta? Doesn't that defeat the purpose of making it fresh?" It's a valid question, and the process might seem a tad counterintuitive. But here's the thing: we're not aiming to dry the pasta completely, just enough to give it a slight firmness that will enhance its cooking process.

- **Maintaining Freshness:** Letting your pasta air-dry doesn't mean you're sacrificing its freshness. We're only talking about a brief drying period, not long enough to lose that fresh taste and texture but just enough to ensure it holds its shape during cooking.
- **Improved Texture and Shape:** Fresh pasta, especially long shapes like spaghetti, can become overly soft and lose its form when boiled immediately after making. By allowing it to dry slightly, you ensure it retains its shape and doesn't turn mushy. For instance, dried spaghetti will hold up much better in boiling water compared to its undried counterpart.
- **Drying Method:** After cutting your fresh pasta into its desired shape, spread it out on a baking tray or a lightly floured surface. It doesn't need long – just about 15 minutes will do the trick. This short drying time is particularly beneficial for long shape pasta.
- **Exceptions to the Rule:** While drying works wonders for many pasta shapes, it's not a one-size-fits-all approach. Stuffed pastas, like ravioli, are an exception. Drying them can compromise the integrity of the dough, making them prone to breaking apart during boiling. So, for these filled delights, it's best to skip the drying step.

Understanding Al Dente

Ah, "Al Dente" – a term that resonates with pasta lovers worldwide. It's an Italian phrase that literally translates to "to the tooth." But when it comes to pasta, it embodies so much more than its literal meaning.

When we say pasta is cooked "Al Dente," we're referring to that perfect point where the pasta is tender yet retains a slight bite. It's neither too soft nor too hard; it's just right. Think of it as the Goldilocks zone of pasta cooking. This texture not only enhances the overall eating experience but also ensures that the pasta is digestible and retains its nutritional value.

Now, when it comes to fresh pasta, there's a twist. The addition of egg and its higher moisture content endow fresh pasta with a bolder flavor and a naturally softer texture. This means it cooks faster than dry pasta. In fact, it's impossible to achieve the traditional "al dente" texture with fresh pasta because it starts off softer even before it meets boiling water.

But why is achieving this texture so crucial, especially for homemade pasta? Fresh pasta, being devoid of any preservatives, has a more delicate structure compared to its store-bought counterparts. It absorbs water quickly, which means there's a fine line between perfectly cooked and overcooked. Striking the right balance ensures that your homemade pasta dishes are not just delicious but also texturally perfect.

Preparing the Water

The water in which the pasta is cooked sets the stage for a perfect performance. Here's how to ensure your water is primed and ready for the task:

- **Quantity Matters:**

For fresh pasta, you don't want to skimp on the water. A generous amount ensures that the pasta has enough room to move around, preventing it from sticking together. A good rule of thumb is to use about 4-5 quarts of water for every pound of pasta.

- **The Importance of a Rolling Boil:**

It's not just about getting the water hot; it's about achieving a consistent, vigorous boil. Those large, lively bubbles that dance across the surface? That's what we're aiming for. This rolling boil guarantees that the pasta cooks evenly, absorbing water at a consistent rate. So, resist the urge to rush this step. After all, perfection is worth the wait.

- **Season Generously with Salt:**

Think of salt as the secret ingredient that elevates the taste of your homemade pasta. As the pasta cooks, it absorbs the salted water, infusing each strand or shape with flavor from within. But timing is everything. Wait until your water is boiling before you add the salt. Why? Because salted water takes its sweet time to boil. As for the quantity, let's take a cue from the Mediterranean. A generous salting ensures that every bite of your pasta is a flavorful journey. I generally recommend using between 2 and 3 tablespoons in 4-5 quarts of water.

Adding and Cooking Pasta

Once your water is boiling and seasoned to perfection, it's time for the main event: introducing your homemade pasta to its hot bath. Here's how to ensure your pasta cooks to perfection:

1. Gently Introduce the Pasta:

Ease your pasta into the boiling water. Whether it's long strands or shaped varieties, ensure they're not clumped together. This will prevent sticking and ensure even cooking. Remember, your homemade pasta is delicate, so treat it with care.

2. Stir Immediately and Regularly:

As soon as your pasta hits the water, stir it. This immediate action, combined with periodic stirring, ensures that each piece remains separate and doesn't stick to the pot or its fellow pasta pieces. While some might suggest adding oil to prevent sticking, a spacious pot and attentive stirring are more effective and recommended.

3. Timing is Everything:

One of the joys of fresh homemade pasta is its swift cooking time. Unlike its store-bought counterpart, which can take upwards of 15 minutes, fresh pasta rarely requires more than 4 minutes in boiling water. However, these times are mere guidelines. Remember, pasta continues to cook a bit when combined with sauce. To truly master the 'al dente' texture, start tasting your pasta about 2 minutes before the suggested cooking time. Repeat this tasting at least three times to ensure you're hitting that perfect texture. After all, pasta deserves all the attention it gets!

4. The Nuances of 'Al Dente':

While we aim for that 'al dente' texture, it's crucial to differentiate between non-filled pasta like spaghetti and filled ones like ravioli. For non-filled varieties, you want to get as close to 'al dente' as possible. However, filled pastas have a different indicator: they're ready when they float to the surface. But be cautious! If they burst open, spilling their filling into the water, they've been overcooked. With non-filled pasta, trust your palate and teeth to guide you.

Draining and Final Touches

After the careful dance of cooking your homemade pasta to perfection, the next steps are crucial to ensure that your dish is both delicious and well-presented. Here's how to masterfully finish off the cooking process:

1. Reserve Some Pasta Water:

Before you even think about draining, always remember to set aside a cup or so of the pasta cooking water. This isn't just any water; it's a starchy elixir that can elevate your sauce. By adding a splash of this reserved water to your sauce, you can achieve a silky texture that allows the sauce to cling beautifully to your pasta.

2. Swift and Gentle Draining:

When your pasta has reached its ideal texture, it's time to drain. Use a colander or a pasta strainer, ensuring you handle the pasta gently to maintain its shape and integrity. Remember, fresh pasta is more delicate than its store-bought counterpart, so treat it with the care it deserves.

3. No Rinsing, Please:

It might be tempting, especially if you're used to cooking store-bought pasta, but resist the urge to rinse your freshly cooked pasta. Rinsing washes away the starchy layer that helps sauces adhere to the pasta, robbing you of maximum flavor.

4. Combining Pasta and Sauce:

Now, it's time to marry your pasta and sauce. Add your drained pasta directly into the pan with your sauce. This not only ensures that every strand or shape is beautifully coated but also allows the flavors to meld. If your sauce is a bit thick, this is the moment to add a splash of the reserved pasta water to achieve the desired consistency.

5. Tossing is Key:

Using a pair of tongs or a large spoon, gently toss your pasta in the sauce. This ensures an even distribution of sauce and lets the flavors truly come together. A well-tossed pasta dish is a joy both visually and gastronomically.

6. Final Seasoning and Garnishing:

Before serving, give your dish a quick taste. Does it need a touch more salt? A sprinkle of freshly ground black pepper? This is also the time to add any final garnishes, be it a sprinkle of freshly grated Parmesan, a drizzle of good quality olive oil, or a scattering of fresh herbs.

HOW TO STORE YOUR PASTA

The aroma of fresh pasta, the soft texture, and the pride of having crafted it with your own hands, it's an experience like no other. But what if you've made a generous batch and can't consume it all at once? Fear not, for storing fresh pasta is simpler than you might think, and with a few tips and tricks, you can enjoy your homemade delicacies for days, or even months, to come.

Short-Term Storage:

Fresh pasta is a delicate beauty, and storing it properly ensures you get the best out of its flavors and textures. If you're gearing up for a meal within the next 1-2 hours, simply cover the pasta with plastic wrap and let it sit at room temperature.

However, life can be unpredictable. Perhaps you've prepared pasta a day in advance for a special occasion, or maybe you've been a tad enthusiastic and made more than you can eat in one go.

In such cases, refrigeration becomes your ally. Before you think of refrigerating your pasta, there's a little trick to ensure it doesn't turn into a sticky mess. Allow the pasta to dry for at least 15 minutes before placing it in the refrigerator. This drying step helps prevent the pasta from sticking together once it's in the container.

Fresh egg pasta can comfortably reside in the refrigerator for 2 to 3 days. However, for the most authentic and vibrant flavors, I'd nudge you to consume it within the first 2 days. To keep it at its best, store the pasta in an airtight container or a sealed plastic bag. While fresh pasta has its charm, it's always best to cook and enjoy it as soon as possible. Beyond a couple of days, the pasta might face issues like oxidation, discoloration, or even sticking together.

Always label your containers with the date you stored the pasta. This way, you can easily keep track of its freshness and ensure you're enjoying it at its prime.

A quick tip: If your pasta starts giving off an unusual or sour aroma, it's signaling that its best days are behind. Watch out for any discoloration, especially a grayish tint. And if it feels a tad too slimy or sticky, even after a generous flour dusting, it's safer and wiser to let it go.

Long-Term Storage:

To preserve its quality beyond a few days, one must consider long-term storage solutions. This not only extends the pasta's usability but also retains its authentic taste and texture. In the realm of long-term storage, two predominant methods stand out: drying and freezing. Each method offers its own set of advantages and considerations, ensuring that the pasta remains as delectable as the day it was made.

- **Drying**

When you've crafted a generous batch of fresh pasta, the joy of having more than you can eat in one sitting is real. But how do you ensure that the remaining pasta remains as delightful as when it was freshly made? Enter the age-old tradition of drying pasta. While fresh pasta is celebrated for its, well, freshness, a little drying doesn't strip it of its essence. However, a word of caution for those who adore filled pastas like ravioli: drying isn't the best method for these treasures. Their fillings, often rich with ingredients that degrade quickly, make them more susceptible to spoilage when dried.

Start by setting up a drying station in your kitchen. A countertop or a large table works wonders. If you're a tad particular like me, lay down a clean kitchen towel or wax paper. As you spread out your pasta, remember to give each piece its space. You wouldn't like being squished in a crowd, and neither does your pasta. This spacing ensures even drying and prevents that dreaded pasta stickiness.

Now, here's a tip from the old books: avoid drafts. While you might enjoy a gentle breeze on a summer day, your pasta prefers calm. Drafts can lead to uneven drying or even cracks. So, keep your pasta away from fans, open windows, or any direct airflow.

Patience, my dear friend, is the name of the game. Depending on where you live and the whims of the weather, drying can take anywhere from 12 to 24 hours. Every few hours, gently turn your pasta, ensuring it dries evenly. And when you think it's ready, do the snap test. Break a piece. If it gives a crisp snap, you're good to go.

Once your pasta has had its sunbath and is all dried up, it's time to store it. Opt for airtight containers. They're your pasta's best friend, keeping out moisture and pests. If you've made a large batch, consider portioning it out. This way, you only expose what you need to air. And always, always label your containers. It's like a timestamp of freshness. While you're at it, make a note to consume the dried pasta within 20 to 30 days, as that's its optimal shelf life.

Find a cool, dark corner for your pasta. Sunlight, heat, and pasta are not the best of friends. And while we're on the topic of what pasta doesn't like, let's talk about freezing. Fresh pasta? Sure, freeze away. But dried pasta prefers the pantry. Freezing can change its texture, and we want to keep it just perfect.

When you're ready to cook your dried pasta, remember it might need a few extra minutes in boiling water compared to its fresh counterpart.

Now, while drying and storing are great ways to prolong the life of your pasta, it's essential to know when it's past its prime. If you notice a change in color, an off smell, or any signs of mold, it's time to bid that batch goodbye. Remember, it's always better to be safe and ensure every pasta dish you serve is of the highest quality.

- **Freezing**

For the forward-thinking chefs who like to plan meals well in advance, freezing is a fantastic option. Fresh pasta freezes beautifully, retaining its flavor and texture. Begin by sprinkling a baking sheet with semola and arrange the individual pieces of pasta in a single layer. This ensures that the pasta doesn't stick to the sheet. After spreading them out, place the sheet in the freezer. It takes about 45 minutes for the pasta to freeze completely, but if you're not in a rush, leaving them overnight won't cause any harm.

Once your pasta pieces are individually frozen, it's time to store them for the long haul. Quickly transfer the pasta to airtight freezer bags, ensuring you don't let them thaw in the process. Gently place the pasta in the bags and seal them airtight. To avoid freezer burn, allow as much air as possible to escape from the bags, but be careful not to break the pasta. If you've made a significant batch and want to store it even longer, consider using an airtight freezer container.

Labeling is crucial. Always label your freezer bags with the date and contents. It's a simple step, but it's one that's often overlooked. Knowing precisely when you prepared the food can be a lifesaver on busy days.

When the craving strikes and you're ready to cook, there's no need to thaw your pasta. Simply toss the frozen pasta directly into boiling water. It will take just 30 seconds to a minute longer than fresh pasta, ensuring you get that perfect al dente bite every time.

However, a word of caution for filled pastas like ravioli: ensure they are well-sealed before freezing to prevent the filling from oozing out during cooking.

In the end, whether you're savoring your pasta immediately or saving it for a special occasion, the key is in the care you take during storage. Fresh pasta is a testament to the time, love, and effort you've invested. With proper storage, you ensure that every bite, whether today or weeks from now, is a delicious tribute to your culinary prowess. So, go forth and store with confidence, knowing that your homemade pasta awaits its moment to shine on your dinner table.

YOUR RECIPE JOURNEY

Welcome to the heart of our culinary adventure, where we'll explore the myriad ways to bring our lovingly crafted pasta to life. As the old Italian saying goes, "A tavola non si invecchia" - At the table, one does not age. And with each bite of these dishes, you'll be transported to moments of pure joy, where time seems to stand still.

Before we dive deep into the world of recipes, let's set the stage. While we've previously delved into the intricate process of making various pasta doughs and shaping them, our focus here will be on the symphony of flavors: the sauces, the seasonings, and the pairings that make our pasta truly shine.

In crafting this collection of recipes, I've sought to bridge the rich culinary traditions of Italy with the diverse tastes of America. It's a reflection of my own journey, being deeply rooted in Italian heritage while embracing the vibrant flavors of the American landscape. By blending these two worlds, we're embarking on a unique gastronomic adventure. Some recipes will feel like a warm embrace from the Italian countryside, while others might surprise you with a twist, resonating with the American palate. This fusion ensures that while we're paying homage to authentic Italian traditions, we're also celebrating the versatility of pasta in contemporary American kitchens. So, whether you're craving the comfort of a classic Italian dish or eager to experiment with a new fusion flavor, there's something here for every palate.

In each category, we've thoughtfully included a brief recap of the pasta-making process. This ensures that as you embark on creating a dish, be it tagliatelle or any other, you have all the essential steps seamlessly integrated, making your culinary experience fluid and delightful.

As we embark on this next chapter of our culinary journey, remember that the essence of cooking lies in the heart. It's about passion, memories, and sharing moments of joy with loved ones. The kitchen is a place of stories, laughter, and dishes that become family legends.

Let's continue our journey, crafting dishes that will be remembered and cherished. Buon appetito!

SPAGHETTI

The very name evokes images of sun-soaked Italian landscapes, bustling kitchens, and families gathering around the dinner table. This long, thin, cylindrical pasta has captured the hearts and palates of people worldwide. Originating from the Italian word "spago," meaning "thin string" or "twine," spaghetti is a testament to the beauty of simplicity in Italian cuisine. The beauty of spaghetti lies in its versatility. Its slender shape makes it the perfect companion for a variety of sauces, from the light and zesty to the rich and hearty.

Spaghetti is a versatile pasta that pairs beautifully with a myriad of flavors. Its delicate nature allows it to meld seamlessly with various sauces, creating a harmonious dish every time.

A tomato-based sauce, whether it's a rich marinara or a hearty Bolognese, complements spaghetti perfectly, offering a delightful tang and depth of flavor. For those who prefer simplicity, an oil-based blend of olive oil, garlic, and a hint of red pepper flakes is a timeless choice, highlighting the pasta's natural taste.

For a taste of the sea, spaghetti and seafood are a match made in culinary heaven. Think of dishes infused with the brininess of clams or mussels, elevated with garlic and white wine. And of course, the fresh and aromatic pesto, with its blend of basil, pine nuts, and Parmesan, adds a burst of summer freshness to the plate.

In short, spaghetti is a canvas waiting for its perfect pairing. As you delve into the upcoming recipes, let your taste buds guide you to create your perfect spaghetti masterpiece.

<u>Step-by-Step Guide:</u>

SERVING: 4-6 people

INGREDIENTS:

- 400 g "Tipo 00" Flour or all-purpose flour
- 228 g Eggs – about four medium eggs

DIRECTIONS:

1. **Mixing the Dough:**
   - On a large, clean work surface or in a large bowl, pour flour into a mound. Create a well in the center that's about 4 inches wide.
   - Gently whisk the eggs using a fork, slowly incorporating the flour from the edges. As the mixture starts coming together, use your hands to fold in the remaining flour until a dough forms.
   - The dough should be firm but not too dry. If it's too sticky, add a sprinkle of flour. If it's too dry and crumbly, you can add a few drops of water.

2. **Kneading:**
   - Press the dough together to form a cohesive ball.
   - Place the dough on a floured surface. Use the heel of your hand to push the dough away from you, then fold it back over itself. Give the dough a quarter turn and repeat for about 8-10 minutes until the dough is smooth and elastic.
   - Once kneaded, shape the dough into a ball and let it rest covered tightly with plastic wrap for at least 30 minutes.

3. **Rolling the Dough:**
   - Divide your dough into manageable pieces, about the size of a lemon and pre-shape it into a rough oval shape.
   - ·Start at the widest setting on your pasta machine.
   - Feed the dough through the rollers. After the first pass, fold the dough in half or into thirds and pass it through the widest setting again.
   - Gradually reduce the roller setting, passing the dough through each time until you reach the desired thickness.

4. **Shaping the Spaghetti:**
   - Set your pasta maker to setting 4 or 5 if you're using a Mercato Atlas, or to setting 3 or 4 if you're using a KitchenAid attachment.
   - Roll the dough through the machine a couple of times to achieve the desired thickness.
   - Place the rolled dough on a floured surface and leave to dry for 10-15 minutes.
   - Attach the spaghetti cutter to your pasta maker.
   - Feed the pasta sheets through the spaghetti attachment.
   - As the spaghetti emerges, collect it in a bowl with a bit of flour, gently tossing to prevent sticking.
   - Lay the finished spaghetti on a dry tea towel.

SPAGHETTI ALLA CARBONARA

SERVES:4-6   PREP: 15 min   COOK: 10 min

INGREDIENTS

For the Dough:
- 400g "Tipo 00" Flour or all-purpose flour
- 228g Eggs – about four medium eggs

For the Seasoning:
- 100g (3.5 oz) Guanciale or Pancetta, diced
- 3 Large Eggs
- 1 cup (100g) Pecorino Romano cheese, grated
- 1 clove Garlic, minced
- Salt and freshly ground Black Pepper, to taste
- 2 tbsp Olive Oil
- Parsley, chopped (for garnish)

TOTAL NUTRITIONAL VALUE

Calories: 2,480; Protein: 92g; Carbohydrates: 320g;
Fat: 92g; Fiber: 10g; Sugar: 8g;

DIRECTIONS

1. Prepare the dough using the listed ingredients and shape into spaghetti following the step-by-step instructions.
2. In a skillet, heat olive oil over medium heat. Add the guanciale or pancetta and cook until it becomes crispy. Add the minced garlic and sauté for a minute.
3. In a bowl, whisk together the eggs, Pecorino Romano cheese, salt, and black pepper.
4. Bring a large pot of salted water to boil. Add spaghetti and cook until al dente. Reserve 1 cup of pasta water and then drain the pasta.
5. Add the drained pasta to the skillet with guanciale. Toss to combine.
6. Remove the skillet from heat and quickly pour in the egg mixture, stirring rapidly to ensure the eggs don't scramble. Add reserved pasta water a little at a time until you get a creamy sauce.
7. Serve immediately, garnished with more Pecorino Romano and chopped parsley.

NOTE

Traditional Carbonara doesn't use cream. The creamy texture comes from the combination of eggs and cheese.

SPAGHETTI WITH MARINARA SAUCE

SERVES:4-6   PREP: 10 min   COOK: 25 min

INGREDIENTS

For the Dough:
- 400g "Tipo 00" Flour or all-purpose flour
- 228g Eggs – about four medium eggs

For the Seasoning:
- 1 can (28 oz) Crushed Tomatoes
- 3 cloves Garlic, minced
- 1 tsp Red Pepper Flakes (optional)
- 2 tbsp Olive Oil
- Salt, to taste
- Fresh Basil Leaves, for garnish
- Grated Parmesan Cheese, for serving

DIRECTIONS

1. Prepare the dough using the listed ingredients and shape into spaghetti following the step-by-step directions.
2. In a saucepan, heat olive oil over medium heat. Add minced garlic and red pepper flakes, sautéing until fragrant.
3. Pour in the crushed tomatoes and season with salt. Let it simmer for 20 minutes, stirring occasionally.
4. In a large pot, bring salted water to a boil. Add spaghetti and cook until al dente. Drain and set aside.
5. Toss the cooked spaghetti in the marinara sauce until well coated.
6. Serve with fresh basil leaves and a sprinkle of grated Parmesan cheese.

TOTAL NUTRITIONAL VALUE

Calories: 2,400; Protein: 60g; Carbohydrates: 320g;
Fat: 60g; Fiber: 20g; Sugar: 40g;

SPAGHETTI WITH GARLIC, CHILI, AND OLIVE OIL

SERVES: 4-6   PREP: 10 min   COOK: 15 min

INGREDIENTS

For the Dough:
- 400g "Tipo 00" Flour or all-purpose flour
- 228g Eggs – about four medium eggs

For the Seasoning:
- 5 cloves Garlic, thinly sliced
- 1 tsp Red Pepper Flakes
- 1/2 cup (120ml) Olive Oil
- Parsley, chopped
- Salt, to taste

DIRECTIONS

1. Prepare the dough using the listed ingredients and shape into spaghetti following the step-by-step Directions.
2. In a large skillet, heat olive oil over medium heat. Add the sliced garlic and red pepper flakes. Sauté until the garlic turns golden but not brown.
3. Bring a large pot of salted water to boil. Add spaghetti and cook until al dente. Drain, reserving 1 cup of pasta water.
4. Add the drained spaghetti to the skillet and toss to coat in the garlic oil. If the pasta seems dry, add a little reserved pasta water.
5. Season with salt and sprinkle with chopped parsley.
6. Serve immediately.

TOTAL NUTRITIONAL VALUE

Calories: 2,080; Protein: 48g; Carbohydrates: 260g; Fat: 120g; Fiber: 8g; Sugar: 4g

NOTE

For an added touch of flavor, you can finish the dish with a sprinkle of grated Parmesan or Pecorino Romano cheese.

SPAGHETTI WITH MEATBALLS

SERVES: 4-6   PREP: 20 min   COOK: 40 min

INGREDIENTS

For the Dough:
- 400g "Tipo 00" Flour or all-purpose flour
- 228g Eggs – about four medium eggs

For the Seasoning:
- 500g (1 lb) Ground Beef
- 1/4 cup (60g) Breadcrumbs
- 1 Large Egg
- 1/4 cup (25g) Grated Parmesan Cheese
- 2 cups (450g) Marinara Sauce (store-bought or homemade)
- 2 cloves Garlic, minced
- 2 tbsp Olive Oil
- Salt and Pepper, to taste
- Fresh Basil or Parsley, for garnish

DIRECTIONS

1. Prepare the dough using the listed ingredients and shape into spaghetti following the step-by-step Directions.
2. In a large bowl, combine ground beef, breadcrumbs, egg, Parmesan cheese, minced garlic, salt, and pepper. Mix until well combined.
3. Form the mixture into meatballs, about the size of a golf ball.
4. In a skillet, heat olive oil over medium heat. Add the meatballs and brown them on all sides.
5. Pour the marinara sauce over the meatballs and let it simmer for 25-30 minutes.
6. Meanwhile, cook the spaghetti in a pot of boiling salted water until al dente. Drain.
7. Serve the meatballs and sauce over the cooked spaghetti. Garnish with fresh basil or parsley and additional grated Parmesan cheese.

TOTAL NUTRITIONAL VALUE

Calories: 3,120; Protein: 210g; Carbohydrates: 280g; Fat: 150g; Fiber: 16g; Sugar: 24g

SPAGHETTI WITH CLAM SAUCE

SERVES:4-6   PREP: 15 min   COOK: 20 min

INGREDIENTS

For the Dough:
- 400g "Tipo 00" Flour or all-purpose flour
- 228g Eggs – about four medium eggs

For the Seasoning:
- 2 cans (6.5 oz each) Chopped Clams, drained with juice reserved
- 4 cloves Garlic, minced
- 1/4 cup (60ml) White Wine
- 1/4 cup (60ml) Olive Oil
- 1 tsp Red Pepper Flakes
- Parsley, chopped
- Salt and Pepper, to taste
- Lemon wedges, for serving

TOTAL NUTRITIONAL VALUE

Calories: 2,280; Protein: 88g; Carbohydrates: 280g; Fat: 80g; Fiber: 8g; Sugar: 8g

DIRECTIONS

1. Prepare the dough using the listed ingredients and shape into spaghetti following the step-by-step Directions.
2. In a skillet, heat olive oil over medium heat. Add minced garlic and red pepper flakes, sautéing until fragrant.
3. Add the white wine and reserved clam juice. Bring to a simmer and let it reduce by half.
4. Add the chopped clams to the skillet and stir to combine.
5. Cook the spaghetti in a pot of boiling salted water until al dente. Drain and add to the skillet, tossing to coat with the clam sauce.
6. Season with salt and pepper. Garnish with chopped parsley.
7. Serve with lemon wedges on the side.

NOTE

Fresh clams can also be used for a more authentic flavor. Just steam them until they open and use the broth in place of the canned clam juice.

SPAGHETTI PUTTANESCA

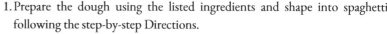

SERVES:4-6   PREP: 15 min   COOK: 25 min

INGREDIENTS

For the Dough:
- 400g "Tipo 00" Flour or all-purpose flour
- 228g Eggs – about four medium eggs

For the Seasoning:
- 1 can (28 oz) Diced Tomatoes
- 1/4 cup (60g) Black Olives, pitted and sliced
- 2 tbsp Capers, drained
- 4 Anchovy Fillets, minced
- 3 cloves Garlic, minced
- 1/4 cup (60ml) Olive Oil
- 1 tsp Red Pepper Flakes
- Parsley, chopped
- Salt, to taste

DIRECTIONS

1. Prepare the dough using the listed ingredients and shape into spaghetti following the step-by-step Directions.
2. In a skillet, heat olive oil over medium heat. Add minced garlic, anchovies, and red pepper flakes. Sauté until the garlic is golden and the anchovies have melted into the oil.
3. Add the diced tomatoes, olives, and capers to the skillet. Let it simmer for 20 minutes.
4. Cook the spaghetti in a pot of boiling salted water until al dente. Drain and add to the skillet, tossing to coat with the puttanesca sauce.
5. Season with salt and garnish with chopped parsley.
6. Serve immediately.

TOTAL NUTRITIONAL VALUE

Calories: 2,160; Protein: 60g; Carbohydrates: 280g; Fat: 88g; Fiber: 16g; Sugar: 20g

NOTE

Puttanesca sauce is known for its bold and briny flavors. Adjust the amount of anchovies, olives, and capers based on your preference.

SPAGHETTI WITH SUN-DRIED TOMATO AND BASIL

SERVES: 4-6   PREP: 15 min   COOK: 15 min

INGREDIENTS

For the Dough:
- 400g "Tipo 00" Flour or all-purpose flour
- 228g Eggs – about four medium eggs

For the Seasoning:
- 1 cup Sun-Dried Tomatoes, chopped
- 1/2 cup (10g) Fresh Basil Leaves, chopped
- 2 cloves Garlic, minced
- 1/4 cup (60ml) Olive Oil
- 1/4 cup (25g) Grated Parmesan Cheese
- 1/4 cup (60ml) Reserved Pasta Water
- Salt and Pepper, to taste
- Crushed Red Pepper Flakes, for a hint of spice (optional)
- Freshly Grated Parmesan Cheese, for serving

DIRECTIONS

1. Prepare the dough using the listed ingredients and shape into spaghetti following the step-by-step Directions.
2. In a large skillet, heat olive oil over medium heat. Add minced garlic and sauté until fragrant.
3. Add the chopped sun-dried tomatoes to the skillet and cook for 2-3 minutes.
4. Add the chopped basil and stir to combine. If the mixture seems too dry, add the reserved pasta water a little at a time until you reach the desired consistency.
5. Cook the spaghetti in a pot of boiling salted water until al dente. Reserve 1/4 cup of pasta water and then drain the spaghetti.
6. Add the cooked spaghetti to the skillet, tossing to coat with the sun-dried tomato and basil mixture.
7. Season with salt, pepper, and crushed red pepper flakes (if using).
8. Serve with a generous sprinkle of freshly grated Parmesan cheese.

TOTAL NUTRITIONAL VALUE

Calories: 2,360; Protein: 68g; Carbohydrates: 280g;
Fat: 112g; Fiber: 16g; Sugar: 24g

NOTE

Sun-dried tomatoes packed in oil can be used for an even richer flavor. Just be sure to drain them well before chopping. If you love a tangy kick, you can also add a splash of balsamic vinegar to the skillet.

SPAGHETTI WITH PESTO AND CHERRY TOMATOES

SERVES: 4-6   PREP: 15 min   COOK: 10 min

INGREDIENTS

For the Dough:
- 400g "Tipo 00" Flour or all-purpose flour
- 228g Eggs – about four medium eggs

For the Seasoning:
- 1 cup (20g) Fresh Basil Pesto (store-bought or homemade)
- 1 cup (150g) Cherry Tomatoes, halved
- 1/4 cup (25g) Grated Parmesan Cheese
- 2 tbsp Olive Oil
- Salt and Pepper, to taste

DIRECTIONS

1. Prepare the dough using the listed ingredients and shape into spaghetti following the step-by-step Directions.
2. Cook the spaghetti in a pot of boiling salted water until al dente. Drain and return to the pot.
3. Add the fresh basil pesto and olive oil to the spaghetti, tossing to coat evenly.
4. Stir in the halved cherry tomatoes.
5. Season with salt and pepper.
6. Serve with a sprinkle of grated Parmesan cheese.

TOTAL NUTRITIONAL VALUE

Calories: 2,320; Protein: 72g; Carbohydrates: 280g;
Fat: 100g; Fiber: 12g; Sugar: 16g;

SPAGHETTI WITH CREAMY LEMON AND SPINACH

SERVES: 4-6   PREP: 15 min   COOK: 15 min

INGREDIENTS

For the Dough:
- 400g "Tipo 00" Flour or all-purpose flour
- 228g Eggs – about four medium eggs

For the Seasoning:
- 2 cups (60-80g= Fresh Spinach, roughly chopped
- 1 cup (240g) Heavy Cream
- Zest and Juice of 1 Lemon
- 2 cloves Garlic, minced
- 2 tbsp Olive Oil
- Salt and Pepper, to taste
- Grated Parmesan Cheese, for serving

DIRECTIONS

1. Prepare the dough using the listed ingredients and shape into spaghetti following the step-by-step Directions.
2. In a skillet, heat olive oil over medium heat. Add minced garlic and sauté until fragrant.
3. Add the heavy cream, lemon zest, and lemon juice. Bring to a gentle simmer.
4. Stir in the chopped spinach and let it wilt.
5. Cook the spaghetti in a pot of boiling salted water until al dente. Drain and add to the skillet, tossing to coat with the creamy lemon and spinach sauce.
6. Season with salt and pepper.
7. Serve with a sprinkle of grated Parmesan cheese.

TOTAL NUTRITIONAL VALUE

Calories: 2,600; Protein: 60g; Carbohydrates: 280g;
Fat: 140g; Fiber: 8g; Sugar: 12g

SPAGHETTI WITH ROASTED RED PEPPER SAUCE

SERVES: 4-6   PREP: 20 min   COOK: 20 min

INGREDIENTS

For the Dough:
- 400g "Tipo 00" Flour or all-purpose flour
- 228g Eggs – about four medium eggs

For the Seasoning:
- 2 Roasted Red Peppers, peeled and chopped
- ½ (120g) cup Heavy Cream
- 2 cloves Garlic, minced
- 2 tbsp Olive Oil
- 1 tsp Smoked Paprika
- Salt and Pepper, to taste
- Fresh Basil, for garnish

DIRECTIONS

1. Prepare the dough using the listed ingredients and shape into spaghetti following the step-by-step Directions.
2. In a blender or food processor, blend the roasted red peppers until smooth.
3. In a skillet, heat olive oil over medium heat. Add minced garlic and sauté until fragrant.
4. Pour in the blended red peppers and heavy cream. Stir in the smoked paprika.
5. Let the sauce simmer for 10 minutes, stirring occasionally.
6. Cook the spaghetti in a pot of boiling salted water until al dente. Drain and add to the skillet, tossing to coat with the roasted red pepper sauce.
7. Season with salt and pepper.
8. Serve garnished with fresh basil leaves.

TOTAL NUTRITIONAL VALUE

Calories: 2,480; Protein: 56g; Carbohydrates: 280g;
Fat: 120g; Fiber: 12g; Sugar: 20g

NOTE

For a smokier flavor, you can roast the red peppers on an open flame until charred. Once cooled, peel off the skin and proceed with the recipe.

TAGLIATELLE

Their name is derived from the Italian verb "tagliare," meaning "to cut," which perfectly describes the process of making these delightful strands. With their delicate texture and ability to hold onto rich sauces, tagliatelle has become a beloved staple in Italian kitchens and beyond.

The beauty of tagliatelle lies in its width and flatness, making it an ideal choice for heavier, meat-based sauces. Think of the classic "Tagliatelle al Ragu," where the pasta's surface beautifully captures every drop of that meaty goodness. But don't let that limit your imagination!

Tagliatelle is equally at home with lighter, cream-based sauces or even a simple toss of olive oil, garlic, and fresh herbs.

Whether you're in the mood for a traditional Bolognese sauce or something more adventurous, tagliatelle offers a versatile canvas for your culinary creations. As we journey through these recipes, let the rich history and tradition of Italian cooking inspire you.

Step-by-Step Guide:

SERVING: 4-6 people

INGREDIENTS:

- 400 g "Tipo 00" Flour or all-purpose flour
- 228 g Eggs – about four medium eggs

DIRECTIONS:

1. **Mixing the Dough:**
   - On a large, clean work surface or in a large bowl, pour flour into a mound. Create a well in the center that's about 4 inches wide.
   - Gently whisk the eggs using a fork, slowly incorporating the flour from the edges. As the mixture starts coming together, use your hands to fold in the remaining flour until a dough forms.
   - The dough should be firm but not too dry. If it's too sticky, add a sprinkle of flour. If it's too dry and crumbly, you can add a few drops of water.

2. **Kneading:**
   - Press the dough together to form a cohesive ball.
   - Place the dough on a floured surface. Use the heel of your hand to push the dough away from you, then fold it back over itself. Give the dough a quarter turn and repeat for about 8-10 minutes until the dough is smooth and elastic.
   - Once kneaded, shape the dough into a ball and let it rest covered tightly with plastic wrap for at least 30 minutes.

3. **Rolling the Dough:**
   - Divide your dough into manageable pieces, about the size of a lemon and pre-shape it into a rough oval shape.
   - Start at the widest setting on your pasta machine.
   - Feed the dough through the rollers. After the first pass, fold the dough in half or into thirds and pass it through the widest setting again.
   - Gradually reduce the roller setting, passing the dough through each time until you reach the desired thickness.

4. **Shaping the Tagliatelle:**
   - Set your pasta maker to setting 4 or 5 if you're using a Mercato Atlas, or to setting 3 or 4 if you're using a KitchenAid attachment.
   - Roll the dough through the machine a couple of times to achieve the desired thickness.
   - Place the rolled dough on a floured surface and leave to dry for 10-15 minutes.
   - Pasta Cutter: Utilize either a straight or serrated pasta cutter to cut the dough sheets into ribbons approximately 8mm wide. For straight lines and uniformity, you may use a ruler if you wish.
   - Sharp Knife: Begin by folding the dough sheets from the shorter sides to form a loose log. Using a sharp knife, cut this dough roll into strands around 8mm in width.
   - Collect the tagliatelle in a bowl with a bit of flour, gently tossing to prevent sticking.
   - Lay the finished pappardelle on a dry tea towel.

TAGLIATELLE WITH BLACK SQUID INK AND GARLIC SHRIMP

SERVES: 4-6   PREP: 40 min   COOK: 25 min

INGREDIENTS

For the Dough:
- 280g "Tipo 00" Flour or all-purpose flour
- 2 whole large eggs (114g)
- 4 yolks from 4 large eggs (72g)
- 4 teaspoons squid ink (about 17g)

For the Seasoning:
- 1 lb (about 500g) large shrimp, peeled and deveined
- 4 garlic cloves, minced
- 1/4 cup (60 ml) extra virgin olive oil
- Red pepper flakes (optional for a touch of heat)
- Salt and pepper to taste
- 1/4 cup (60 ml) white wine
- Fresh parsley, chopped, for garnish

TOTAL NUTRITIONAL VALUE

Calories: 2,200; Protein: 140g; Carbohydrates: 280g; Fat: 60g; Fiber: 5g; Sugar: 5g

DIRECTIONS

1. Prepare the dough using the listed ingredients and shape into tagliatelle following the step-by-step Directions.
2. In a large skillet, heat the olive oil over medium heat. Add the minced garlic and red pepper flakes (if using) and sauté until fragrant, about 1 minute.
3. Add the shrimp to the skillet and season with salt and pepper. Cook until the shrimp turn pink on both sides, about 2-3 minutes per side.
4. Pour in the white wine and let it simmer for 2 minutes, allowing the alcohol to evaporate.
5. Meanwhile, cook the black squid ink tagliatelle in a large pot of boiling salted water until al dente.
6. Before draining the pasta, reserve about 1/2 cup (120 ml) of the cooking water.
7. Drain and add to the skillet with the shrimp.
8. Toss the pasta well to coat with the garlic shrimp mixture. If the sauce is too thick or if you desire a creamier consistency, gradually add the reserved cooking water until you reach the desired consistency.
9. Serve hot, garnished with chopped fresh parsley.

TAGLIATELLE ALLA BOLOGNESE

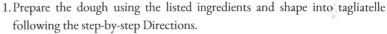
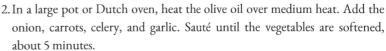

SERVES: 4-6   PREP: 30 min   COOK: 2 hours

INGREDIENTS

For the Dough:
- 400g "Tipo 00" Flour or all-purpose flour
- 228g Eggs – about four medium eggs

For the Seasoning:
- 1 lb (about 500g) ground beef
- 1 onion, finely chopped
- 2 carrots, finely chopped
- 2 celery stalks, finely chopped
- 3 garlic cloves, minced
- 1/4 cup (60 ml) extra virgin olive oil
- 1 cup (240 ml) red wine
- 1 can (28 oz or 800g) crushed tomatoes
- Salt and pepper to taste
- 1/4 cup (60 ml) whole milk or heavy cream
- Freshly grated Parmesan cheese, for serving

TOTAL NUTRITIONAL VALUE

Calories: 2,800; Protein: 150g; Carbohydrates: 300g; Fat: 100g; Fiber: 20g; Sugar: 20g

DIRECTIONS

1. Prepare the dough using the listed ingredients and shape into tagliatelle following the step-by-step Directions.
2. In a large pot or Dutch oven, heat the olive oil over medium heat. Add the onion, carrots, celery, and garlic. Sauté until the vegetables are softened, about 5 minutes.
3. Add the ground beef to the pot, breaking it apart with a spoon. Cook until browned.
4. Pour in the red wine and let it simmer until reduced by half.
5. Add the crushed tomatoes and season with salt and pepper. Reduce the heat to low and let the sauce simmer for 1.5 hours, stirring occasionally.
6. Stir in the milk or heavy cream and cook for an additional 10 minutes.
7. Meanwhile, cook the tagliatelle in a large pot of boiling salted water until al dente. Drain and add to the pot with the Bolognese sauce.
8. Toss the pasta well to coat with the sauce. Serve hot, garnished with freshly grated Parmesan cheese.

NOTE

Bolognese sauce is a rich and hearty meat sauce. For a creamier texture, you can increase the amount of milk or heavy cream. Adjust salt and pepper to taste.

SPINACH TAGLIATELLE WITH ALFREDO SAUCE

SERVES: 4-6   PREP: 35 min   COOK: 20 min

INGREDIENTS

For the Dough:
- 280g "Tipo 00" Flour or all-purpose flour
- 5 yolks from 5 large eggs (90g)
- 1 whole large egg (57g)
- 56g spinach purée

For the Seasoning:
- 1 cup (240 ml) heavy cream
- 1/2 cup (115g) unsalted butter
- 1 cup (100g) freshly grated Parmesan cheese
- Salt and freshly ground black pepper, to taste
- Freshly grated nutmeg, optional

DIRECTIONS

1. Prepare the dough using the listed ingredients and shape into tagliatelle following the step-by-step Directions.
2. In a saucepan, melt the butter over medium heat. Add the heavy cream and bring to a gentle simmer.
3. Reduce the heat to low and whisk in the Parmesan cheese until melted and the sauce is smooth.
4. Season with salt, black pepper, and a pinch of nutmeg (if using). Keep warm.
5. Cook the green spinach tagliatelle in a large pot of boiling salted water until al dente. Drain and add to the saucepan with the Alfredo sauce.
6. Toss the pasta well to coat with the sauce. Serve immediately.

TOTAL NUTRITIONAL VALUE

Calories: 2,500; Protein: 80g; Carbohydrates: 260g;
Fat: 140g; Fiber: 6g; Sugar: 8g

BEET TAGLIATELLE WITH RICOTTA AND TOASTED WALNUTS

SERVES: 4-6   PREP: 40 min   COOK: 20 min

INGREDIENTS

For the Dough:
- 280g "Tipo 00" Flour or all-purpose flour
- 5 yolks from 5 large eggs (90g)
- 1 whole large egg (57g)
- 56g beet purée

For the Seasoning:
- 1 cup (250g) ricotta cheese
- 1/2 cup (60g) toasted walnuts, roughly chopped
- 1/4 cup (60 ml) extra virgin olive oil
- Salt and freshly ground black pepper, to taste
- Fresh basil or mint leaves, for garnish

DIRECTIONS

1. Prepare the dough using the listed ingredients and shape into tagliatelle following the step-by-step Directions.
2. In a large bowl, combine the ricotta cheese, toasted walnuts, and olive oil. Season with salt and black pepper. Mix well.
3. Cook the purple-red beet tagliatelle in a large pot of boiling salted water until al dente. Drain and add to the bowl with the ricotta mixture.
4. Toss the pasta well to coat with the ricotta and walnuts. Serve immediately, garnished with fresh basil or mint leaves.

TOTAL NUTRITIONAL VALUE

Calories: 2,300; Protein: 70g; Carbohydrates: 240g;
Fat: 130g; Fiber: 8g; Sugar: 10g

TAGLIATELLE WITH CHICKEN AND MUSHROOM CREAM SAUCE

SERVES: 4-6   PREP: 20 min   COOK: 30 min

INGREDIENTS

For the Dough:
- 400g "Tipo 00" Flour or all-purpose flour
- 228g Eggs – about four medium eggs

For the Seasoning:
- 2 chicken breasts, thinly sliced
- 1 cup (about 150g) mushrooms, sliced
- 1 onion, finely chopped
- 2 garlic cloves, minced
- 1/4 cup (60 ml) white wine (optional)
- 1 cup (240 ml) heavy cream
- 1/4 cup (60 ml) chicken broth or stock
- 2 tbsp olive oil
- Salt and freshly ground black pepper, to taste
- Fresh parsley, chopped, for garnish

DIRECTIONS

1. Prepare the dough using the listed ingredients and shape into tagliatelle following the step-by-step Directions.
2. In a large skillet, heat olive oil over medium heat. Add the chicken slices and cook until browned on both sides. Remove from the skillet and set aside.
3. In the same skillet, add the onions and garlic. Sauté until translucent. Add the mushrooms and cook until they release their moisture.
4. Pour in the white wine (if using) and let it reduce by half. Add the chicken broth or stock and heavy cream. Bring to a simmer.
5. Return the cooked chicken slices to the skillet and let it simmer in the sauce for 5 minutes.
6. Meanwhile, cook the tagliatelle in a large pot of boiling salted water until al dente. Drain and add to the skillet with the chicken and mushroom cream sauce.
7. Toss the pasta well to coat with the sauce. Season with salt and pepper. Serve garnished with chopped fresh parsley.

TOTAL NUTRITIONAL VALUE

Calories: 2,600; Protein: 110g; Carbohydrates: 270g; Fat: 130g; Fiber: 8g; Sugar: 6g

TAGLIATELLE WITH WALNUT AND ARUGULA PESTO

SERVES: 4-6   PREP: 20 min   COOK: 15 min

INGREDIENTS

For the Dough:
- 400g "Tipo 00" Flour or all-purpose flour
- 228g Eggs – about four medium eggs

For the Seasoning:
- 1 cup (about 30g) fresh arugula
- 1/2 cup (about 60g) walnuts, toasted
- 1/2 cup (50g) freshly grated Parmesan cheese
- 1 garlic clove
- 1/2 cup (120 ml) extra virgin olive oil
- Salt and freshly ground black pepper, to taste
- Lemon zest, for garnish (optional)

DIRECTIONS

1. Prepare the dough using the listed ingredients and shape into tagliatelle following the step-by-step Directions.
2. In a food processor, combine the arugula, toasted walnuts, Parmesan cheese, and garlic. Pulse until finely chopped.
3. With the processor running, slowly pour in the olive oil until the mixture becomes a smooth paste. Season with salt and pepper.
4. Cook the tagliatelle in a large pot of boiling salted water until al dente. Drain, reserving 1/4 cup of pasta water.
5. In a large bowl, combine the tagliatelle with the walnut and arugula pesto. Add a bit of the reserved pasta water if needed to make the sauce smoother.
6. Toss well to coat the pasta with the pesto. Serve with a sprinkle of lemon zest (if using).

TOTAL NUTRITIONAL VALUE

Calories: 2,400; Protein: 80g; Carbohydrates: 250g; Fat: 140g; Fiber: 10g; Sugar: 5g

TAGLIATELLE WITH SAUSAGE AND BROCCOLI RABE

SERVES: 4-6   PREP: 20 min   COOK: 30 min

INGREDIENTS

For the Dough:
- 400g "Tipo 00" Flour or all-purpose flour
- 228g Eggs – about four medium eggs

For the Seasoning:
- 1 lb (about 450g) Italian sausage, casings removed and crumbled
- 1 bunch broccoli rabe, trimmed and roughly chopped
- 3 garlic cloves, minced
- 1/4 teaspoon red pepper flakes (adjust to taste)
- 1/4 cup (60 ml) extra virgin olive oil
- Salt and freshly ground black pepper, to taste
- Grated Parmesan cheese, for serving

TOTAL NUTRITIONAL VALUE

Calories: 2,500; Protein: 90g; Carbohydrates: 260g;
Fat: 140g; Fiber: 10g; Sugar: 4g;

DIRECTIONS

1. Prepare the dough using the listed ingredients and shape into tagliatelle following the step-by-step Directions.
2. In a large skillet, heat olive oil over medium heat. Add the crumbled sausage and cook until browned. Remove from the skillet and set aside.
3. In the same skillet, add more olive oil if needed, then sauté garlic and red pepper flakes until fragrant.
4. Add the chopped broccoli rabe and sauté until tender, about 5-7 minutes.
5. Return the cooked sausage to the skillet and mix well.
6. Meanwhile, cook the tagliatelle in a large pot of boiling salted water until al dente. Before draining the pasta, reserve about 1/2 cup (120 ml) of the cooking water.
7. Drain the fettuccine and add to the skillet with the sausage and broccoli rabe mixture. Toss well to combine.
8. If the mixture is too dry or if you desire a glossier sauce, gradually add the reserved cooking water until you reach the desired consistency.
9. Season with salt and pepper. Serve with grated Parmesan cheese on top.

TOMATO TAGLIATELLE WITH PROSCIUTTO, ASPARAGUS, AND PARMESAN

SERVES: 4-6   PREP: 40 min   COOK: 30 min

INGREDIENTS

For the Dough:
- 280g "Tipo 00" Flour or all-purpose flour
- 5 yolks from 5 large eggs (90g)
- 1 whole large egg (57g)
- 56g tomato paste

For the Seasoning:
- 6 slices of prosciutto, torn into pieces
- 1 bunch of asparagus (about 250g), trimmed and cut into 2-inch pieces
- 1/2 cup (50g) freshly grated Parmesan cheese
- 3 garlic cloves, minced
- 1/4 cup (60 ml) extra virgin olive oil
- Salt and freshly ground black pepper, to taste
- Fresh basil leaves, for garnish

TOTAL NUTRITIONAL VALUE

Calories: 2,400; Protein: 100g; Carbohydrates: 290g; Fat: 80g; Fiber: 7g; Sugar: 8g

DIRECTIONS

1. Prepare the dough using the listed ingredients and shape into tagliatelle following the step-by-step Directions.
2. In a large skillet, heat olive oil over medium heat. Add the minced garlic and sauté until fragrant.
3. Add the asparagus pieces to the skillet and cook until they are tender but still have a slight bite.
4. Add the torn prosciutto pieces and toss to combine.
5. Meanwhile, cook the orange tomato tagliatelle in a large pot of boiling salted water until al dente. Drain and add to the skillet with the asparagus and prosciutto.
6. Toss the pasta well to combine. Season with salt and pepper. Serve topped with freshly grated Parmesan cheese and garnished with fresh basil leaves.

TAGLIATELLE WITH SUN-DRIED TOMATOES AND OLIVES

SERVES: 4-6   PREP: 20 min   COOK: 25 min

INGREDIENTS

For the Dough:
- 400g "Tipo 00" Flour or all-purpose flour
- 228g Eggs – about four medium eggs

For the Seasoning:
- 1 cup (150g) sun-dried tomatoes, chopped
- 1/2 cup (90g) black olives, pitted and sliced
- 3 garlic cloves, minced
- 1/4 cup (60 ml) extra virgin olive oil
- 1/4 teaspoon red pepper flakes (optional)
- Salt and freshly ground black pepper, to taste
- Fresh basil leaves, chopped, for garnish
- Grated Parmesan cheese, for serving

DIRECTIONS

1. Prepare the dough using the listed ingredients and shape into tagliatelle following the step-by-step Directions.
2. In a large skillet, heat olive oil over medium heat. Add the minced garlic and sauté until fragrant.
3. Add the chopped sun-dried tomatoes and sliced olives to the skillet, stirring to combine.
4. Meanwhile, cook the tagliatelle in a large pot of boiling salted water until al dente. Before draining the pasta, reserve about 1/2 cup (120 ml) of the cooking water.
5. Drain the tagliatelle and add to the skillet with the tomato and olive mixture.
6. Toss the pasta well to combine. If the mixture is too dry or if you desire a glossier sauce, gradually add the reserved cooking water until you reach the desired consistency.
7. Serve immediately, garnished with fresh basil leaves and freshly grated Parmesan cheese.

TOTAL NUTRITIONAL VALUE

Calories: 2,200; Protein: 70g; Carbohydrates: 280g; Fat: 80g; Fiber: 8g; Sugar: 7g

TAGLIATELLE WITH ROASTED VEGETABLES AND OLIVE OIL

SERVES: 4-6   PREP: 25 min   COOK: 40 min

INGREDIENTS

For the Dough:
- 400g "Tipo 00" Flour or all-purpose flour
- 228g Eggs – about four medium eggs

For the Seasoning:
- 1 cup (150g) bell peppers (red, yellow, and/or green), sliced
- 1 zucchini, sliced
- 1 red onion, sliced
- 1/4 cup (60 ml) extra virgin olive oil, plus more for drizzling
- Salt and freshly ground black pepper, to taste
- Fresh rosemary leaves, chopped, for garnish
- Grated Parmesan cheese, for serving

DIRECTIONS

1. Preheat the oven to 425°F (220°C). Place the sliced bell peppers, zucchini, and red onion on a baking sheet. Drizzle with olive oil and season with salt and pepper. Roast in the oven for about 20 minutes or until the vegetables are tender and slightly caramelized.
2. Prepare the dough using the listed ingredients and shape into tagliatelle following the step-by-step Directions.
3. Cook the tagliatelle in a large pot of boiling salted water until al dente. Before draining the pasta, reserve about 1/2 cup (120 ml) of the cooking water.
4. Drain the tagliatelle and transfer to a large serving bowl.
5. Add the roasted vegetables to the pasta and toss to combine. Drizzle with additional olive oil if desired. If the mixture is too dry or if you desire a glossier sauce, gradually add the reserved cooking water until you reach the desired consistency.
6. Season with salt and pepper. Serve garnished with chopped fresh rosemary leaves and freshly grated Parmesan cheese.

TOTAL NUTRITIONAL VALUE

Calories: 2,100; Protein: 60g; Carbohydrates: 280g; Fat: 70g; Fiber: 9g; Sugar: 8g;

FETTUCCINE

Emerging from the heart of Italy, fettuccine has graced our tables with its broad and flat elegance. The name itself, derived from the Italian word "fettuccia," meaning "small ribbon," perfectly captures its essence.

Originating primarily from the regions of Tuscany and Lazio, fettuccine has become synonymous with the classic "Alfredo" sauce, a creamy delight that clings to each strand, ensuring a rich bite every time.

However, its versatility doesn't stop there. Fettuccine's width makes it a prime candidate for robust meat sauces, yet it's delicate enough to dance with lighter, herb-infused concoctions.

As we delve into the recipes that follow, let the timeless charm of fettuccine guide your culinary explorations, reminding you of the rich tapestry of Italian gastronomy.

<u>Step-by-Step Guide:</u>

SERVING: 4-6 people

INGREDIENTS:

- 400 g "Tipo 00" Flour or all-purpose flour
- 228 g Eggs – about four medium eggs

DIRECTIONS:

1. **Mixing the Dough:**
   - On a large, clean work surface or in a large bowl, pour flour into a mound. Create a well in the center that's about 4 inches wide.
   - Gently whisk the eggs using a fork, slowly incorporating the flour from the edges. As the mixture starts coming together, use your hands to fold in the remaining flour until a dough forms.
   - The dough should be firm but not too dry. If it's too sticky, add a sprinkle of flour. If it's too dry and crumbly, you can add a few drops of water.

2. **Kneading:**
   - Press the dough together to form a cohesive ball.
   - Place the dough on a floured surface. Use the heel of your hand to push the dough away from you, then fold it back over itself. Give the dough a quarter turn and repeat for about 8-10 minutes until the dough is smooth and elastic.
   - Once kneaded, shape the dough into a ball and let it rest covered tightly with plastic wrap for at least 30 minutes.

3. **Rolling the Dough:**
   - Divide your dough into manageable pieces, about the size of a lemon and pre-shape it into a rough oval shape.
   - Start at the widest setting on your pasta machine.
   - Feed the dough through the rollers. After the first pass, fold the dough in half or into thirds and pass it through the widest setting again.
   - Gradually reduce the roller setting, passing the dough through each time until you reach the desired thickness.

4. **Shaping the Fettuccine:**
   - Set your pasta maker to setting 6 or 7 if you're using a Mercato Atlas, or to setting 5 or 6 if you're using a KitchenAid attachment.
   - Roll the dough through the machine a couple of times to achieve the desired thickness.
   - Place the rolled dough on a floured surface and leave to dry for 10-15 minutes.
   - Attach the fettuccine cutter to your pasta maker.
   - Feed the pasta sheets through the fettuccine attachment.
   - As the fettucine emerges, collect it in a bowl with a bit of flour, gently tossing to prevent sticking.
   - Lay the finished fettucine on a dry tea towel.

FETTUCCINE WITH BLACK SQUID INK AND MUSSELS

SERVES: 4-6   PREP: 40 min   COOK: 30 min

INGREDIENTS

For the Dough:
- 280g "Tipo 00" Flour or all-purpose flour
- 2 whole large eggs (114g)
- 4 yolks from 4 large eggs (72g)
- 4 teaspoons squid ink (about 17g)

For the Seasoning:
- 1 lb (about 450g) fresh mussels, cleaned and debearded
- 3 garlic cloves, minced
- 1/4 cup (60 ml) white wine
- 1/4 cup (60 ml) extra virgin olive oil
- 1/4 teaspoon red pepper flakes (optional)
- Salt and freshly ground black pepper, to taste
- Fresh parsley, chopped, for garnish
- Lemon wedges, for serving

TOTAL NUTRITIONAL VALUE

Calories: 2,300; Protein: 120g; Carbohydrates:
280g; Fat: 70g; Fiber: 5g; Sugar: 5g

DIRECTIONS

1. Prepare the dough using the listed ingredients and shape into fettuccine following the step-by-step Directions.
2. In a large skillet, heat olive oil over medium-high heat. Add the minced garlic and red pepper flakes (if using) and sauté until fragrant.
3. Add the mussels and white wine to the skillet. Cover and cook until the mussels have opened, about 5-7 minutes. Discard any mussels that do not open.
4. Meanwhile, cook the black squid ink fettuccine in a large pot of boiling salted water until al dente. Drain and add to the skillet with the mussels.
5. Toss the pasta well to coat with the mussels and their juices. Season with salt and pepper. Serve garnished with chopped fresh parsley and lemon wedges on the side.

FETTUCCINE ALFREDO (CLASSIC CREAM AND PARMESAN SAUCE)

SERVES: 4-6   PREP: 15 min   COOK: 20 min

INGREDIENTS

For the Dough:
- 400g "Tipo 00" Flour or all-purpose flour
- 228g Eggs – about four medium eggs

For the Seasoning:
- 1 cup (240 ml) heavy cream
- 1/2 cup (115g) unsalted butter
- 1 cup (100g) freshly grated Parmesan cheese
- Salt and freshly ground black pepper, to taste
- Fresh parsley, chopped, for garnish (optional)

DIRECTIONS

1. Prepare the dough using the listed ingredients and shape into fettuccine following the step-by-step Directions.
2. In a large skillet or saucepan, melt the butter over medium heat. Add the heavy cream and bring to a gentle simmer.
3. Reduce the heat to low and gradually whisk in the grated Parmesan cheese until the sauce is smooth and creamy. Season with salt and pepper.
4. Cook the fettuccine in a large pot of boiling salted water until al dente. Drain and add to the skillet with the Alfredo sauce.
5. Toss the pasta well to coat with the sauce. Serve immediately, garnished with chopped fresh parsley if desired.

TOTAL NUTRITIONAL VALUE

Calories: 2,800; Protein: 90g; Carbohydrates: 290g;
Fat: 160g; Fiber: 5g; Sugar: 6g

SPINACH FETTUCCINE WITH SALMON AND DILL

SERVES: 4-6   PREP: 40 min   COOK: 30 min

INGREDIENTS

For the Dough:
- 280g "Tipo 00" Flour or all-purpose flour
- 5 yolks from 5 large eggs (90g)
- 1 whole large egg (57g)
- 56g spinach purée
- For the spinach purée: 1 bunch fresh spinach (about 280g), rinsed and stems trimmed

For the Seasoning:
- 2 salmon fillets (about 400g), skin removed and diced
- 2 tablespoons fresh dill, chopped
- 3 garlic cloves, minced
- 1/4 cup (60 ml) extra virgin olive oil
- 1/4 cup (60 ml) white wine
- Salt and freshly ground black pepper, to taste
- Lemon wedges, for serving

TOTAL NUTRITIONAL VALUE

Calories: 2,400; Protein: 140g; Carbohydrates: 280g; Fat: 80g; Fiber: 6g; Sugar: 5g

DIRECTIONS

1. Prepare the dough using the listed ingredients and shape into fettuccine following the step-by-step Directions.
2. In a large skillet, heat olive oil over medium heat. Add the minced garlic and sauté until fragrant.
3. Add the diced salmon to the skillet and cook until lightly browned and cooked through.
4. Pour in the white wine and let it simmer until reduced by half.
5. Meanwhile, cook the spinach fettuccine in a large pot of boiling salted water until al dente. Before draining the pasta, reserve about 1/2 cup (120 ml) of the cooking water.
6. Drain the fettuccine and add to the skillet with the salmon mixture. If the mixture is too dry or if you desire a glossier sauce, gradually add the reserved cooking water until you reach the desired consistency.
7. Serve with lemon wedges on the side.

BEET FETTUCCINE WITH PROSCIUTTO AND FETA

SERVES: 4-6   PREP: 40 min   COOK: 25 min

INGREDIENTS

For the Dough:
- 280g "Tipo 00" Flour or all-purpose flour
- 5 yolks from 5 large eggs (90g)
- 1 whole large egg (57g)
- 56g beet purée
- For the beet purée: 2 small beets (about 200g), rinsed and trimmed

For the Seasoning:
- 6 slices of prosciutto, torn into pieces
- 1 cup (150g) feta cheese, crumbled
- 2 garlic cloves, minced
- 1/4 cup (60 ml) extra virgin olive oil
- Salt and freshly ground black pepper, to taste
- Fresh basil leaves, for garnish

TOTAL NUTRITIONAL VALUE

Calories: 2,300; Protein: 90g; Carbohydrates: 280g; Fat: 90g; Fiber: 6g; Sugar: 8g

DIRECTIONS

1. Prepare the dough using the listed ingredients and shape into fettuccine following the step-by-step Directions.
2. In a large skillet, heat olive oil over medium heat. Add the minced garlic and sauté until fragrant.
3. Add the torn prosciutto pieces to the skillet and cook until they are slightly crispy.
4. Meanwhile, cook the purple-red beet fettuccine in a large pot of boiling salted water until al dente. Drain and add to the skillet with the prosciutto.
5. Toss the pasta well to combine. Remove from heat and stir in the crumbled feta cheese. Season with salt and pepper. Serve garnished with fresh basil leaves.

FETTUCCINE WITH CREAMY MUSHROOM AND THYME SAUCE

SERVES: 4-6 PREP: 20 min COOK: 30 min

INGREDIENTS

For the Dough:
- 400g "Tipo 00" Flour or all-purpose flour
- 228g Eggs – about four medium eggs

For the Seasoning:
- 2 cups (about 200g) mixed mushrooms (like cremini, shiitake, and portobello), sliced
- 1 cup (240 ml) heavy cream
- 3 garlic cloves, minced
- 2 tablespoons fresh thyme leaves, chopped
- 1/4 cup (60 ml) extra virgin olive oil
- Salt and freshly ground black pepper, to taste
- Grated Parmesan cheese, for serving

DIRECTIONS

1. Prepare the dough using the listed ingredients and shape into fettuccine following the step-by-step Directions.
2. In a large skillet, heat olive oil over medium heat. Add the minced garlic and sauté until fragrant.
3. Add the sliced mushrooms to the skillet and cook until they release their moisture and become tender.
4. Pour in the heavy cream and bring to a gentle simmer. Stir in the chopped thyme and season with salt and pepper.
5. Cook the fettuccine in a large pot of boiling salted water until al dente. Drain and add to the skillet with the creamy mushroom sauce.
6. Toss the pasta well to combine. Serve topped with freshly grated Parmesan cheese.

TOTAL NUTRITIONAL VALUE

Calories: 2,500; Protein: 80g; Carbohydrates: 290g;
Fat: 130g; Fiber: 6g; Sugar: 7g

TOMATO FETTUCCINE WITH MEDITERRANEAN TUNA AND CAPERS

SERVES: 4-6 PREP: 40 min COOK: 25 min

INGREDIENTS

For the Dough:
- 280g "Tipo 00" Flour or all-purpose flour
- 5 yolks from 5 large eggs (90g)
- 1 whole large egg (57g)
- 56g tomato paste

For the Seasoning:
- 1 can (5 oz or 142g) tuna in olive oil, drained and flaked
- 2 tablespoons capers, drained
- 1/4 cup (60 ml) extra virgin olive oil
- 3 garlic cloves, minced
- 1/4 teaspoon red pepper flakes (optional)
- Salt and freshly ground black pepper, to taste
- Fresh parsley, chopped, for garnish
- Lemon wedges, for serving

DIRECTIONS

1. Prepare the dough using the listed ingredients and shape into fettuccine following the step-by-step Directions.
2. In a large skillet, heat olive oil over medium heat. Add the minced garlic and red pepper flakes (if using) and sauté until fragrant.
3. Stir in the flaked tuna and capers, cooking for a few minutes to combine the flavors.
4. Meanwhile, cook the orange tomato fettuccine in a large pot of boiling salted water until al dente. Before draining the pasta, reserve about 1/2 cup (120 ml) of the cooking water.
5. Drain the fettuccine and add to the skillet with the tuna and caper mixture. If the mixture is too dry or if you desire a glossier sauce, gradually add the reserved cooking water until you reach the desired consistency.
6. Serve garnished with chopped fresh parsley and lemon wedges on the side.

TOTAL NUTRITIONAL VALUE

Calories: 2,200; Protein: 90g; Carbohydrates: 280g;
Fat: 70g; Fiber: 6g; Sugar: 6g

FETTUCCINE WITH SAUSAGE AND BELL PEPPERS

SERVES:4-6 PREP: 20 min COOK: 30 min

INGREDIENTS

For the Dough:
- 400g "Tipo 00" Flour or all-purpose flour
- 228g Eggs – about four medium eggs

For the Seasoning:
- 1 lb (450g) Italian sausage, casings removed
- 2 bell peppers (1 red and 1 yellow), thinly sliced
- 3 garlic cloves, minced
- 1/4 cup (60 ml) extra virgin olive oil
- Salt and freshly ground black pepper, to taste
- Fresh basil or parsley, chopped, for garnish
- Grated Parmesan cheese, for serving

DIRECTIONS

1. Prepare the dough using the listed ingredients and shape into fettuccine following the step-by-step Directions.
2. In a large skillet, heat olive oil over medium heat. Add the minced garlic and sauté until fragrant.
3. Add the sausage to the skillet, breaking it up with a spoon, and cook until browned.
4. Stir in the sliced bell peppers and cook until they are tender.
5. Meanwhile, cook the fettuccine in a large pot of boiling salted water until al dente. Before draining the pasta, reserve about 1/2 cup (120 ml) of the cooking water.
6. Drain the fettuccine and add to the skillet with the sausage and bell peppers. If the mixture is too dry or if you desire a glossier sauce, gradually add the reserved cooking water until you reach the desired consistency.
7. Season with salt and pepper. Serve garnished with chopped fresh basil or parsley and freshly grated Parmesan cheese.

TOTAL NUTRITIONAL VALUE

Calories: 2,600; Protein: 100g; Carbohydrates: 290g; Fat: 130g; Fiber: 6g; Sugar: 8g

FETTUCCINE WITH SAUSAGE AND FENNEL RAGU

SERVES:4-6 PREP: 25 min COOK: 40 min

INGREDIENTS

For the Dough:
- 400g "Tipo 00" Flour or all-purpose flour
- 228g Eggs – about four medium eggs

For the Seasoning:
- 1 lb (450g) Italian sausage, casings removed
- 1 large fennel bulb, thinly sliced
- 1 can (28 oz) crushed tomatoes
- 3 garlic cloves, minced
- 1/4 cup (60 ml) extra virgin olive oil
- Salt and freshly ground black pepper, to taste
- Fresh fennel fronds, chopped, for garnish
- Grated Parmesan cheese, for serving

DIRECTIONS

1. Prepare the dough using the listed ingredients and shape into fettuccine following the step-by-step Directions.
2. In a large skillet, heat olive oil over medium heat. Add the minced garlic and sauté until fragrant.
3. Add the sausage to the skillet, breaking it up with a spoon, and cook until browned.
4. Stir in the sliced fennel and cook until it begins to soften.
5. Add the crushed tomatoes to the skillet, reduce the heat to low, and let the ragu simmer for about 20 minutes.
6. Meanwhile, cook the fettuccine in a large pot of boiling salted water until al dente. Before draining the pasta, reserve about 1/2 cup (120 ml) of the cooking water.
7. Drain the fettuccine and add to the skillet with the sausage and fennel ragu. If the sauce is too thick or if you desire a creamier consistency, gradually add the reserved cooking water until you reach the desired consistency.
8. Season with salt and pepper. Serve garnished with chopped fresh fennel fronds and freshly grated Parmesan cheese.

TOTAL NUTRITIONAL VALUE

Calories: 2,700; Protein: 110g; Carbohydrates: 300g; Fat: 135g; Fiber: 7g; Sugar: 9g

FETTUCCINE WITH PESTO AND GRILLED VEGETABLES

SERVES: 4-6   PREP: 25 min   COOK: 35 min

INGREDIENTS

For the Dough:
- 400g "Tipo 00" Flour or all-purpose flour
- 228g Eggs – about four medium eggs

For the Seasoning:
- 1 cup (240 ml) basil pesto (store-bought or homemade)
- 1 zucchini, sliced lengthwise
- 1 bell pepper, sliced into large pieces
- 1 red onion, sliced into thick rings
- 1/4 cup (60 ml) extra virgin olive oil
- Salt and freshly ground black pepper, to taste
- Grated Parmesan cheese, for serving

TOTAL NUTRITIONAL VALUE

Calories: 2,500; Protein: 80g; Carbohydrates: 280g;
Fat: 130g; Fiber: 8g; Sugar: 7g

DIRECTIONS

1. Prepare the dough using the listed ingredients and shape into fettuccine following the step-by-step Directions.
2. Preheat a grill or grill pan over medium-high heat. Brush the vegetables with olive oil and season with salt and pepper. Grill the vegetables until they are tender and have grill marks, turning occasionally.
3. Once grilled, remove the vegetables and chop them into bite-sized pieces.
4. Meanwhile, cook the fettuccine in a large pot of boiling salted water until al dente. Before draining the pasta, reserve about 1/2 cup (120 ml) of the cooking water.
5. Drain the fettuccine and return it to the pot. Stir in the pesto and grilled vegetables. If the mixture is too thick or if you desire a glossier sauce, gradually add the reserved cooking water until you reach the desired consistency.
6. Season with additional salt and pepper if needed. Serve topped with freshly grated Parmesan cheese.

FETTUCCINE WITH SHRIMP AND LEMON BUTTER SAUCE

SERVES: 4-6   PREP: 20 min   COOK: 30 min

INGREDIENTS

For the Dough:
- 400g "Tipo 00" Flour or all-purpose flour
- 228g Eggs – about four medium eggs

For the Seasoning:
- 1 lb (450g) large shrimp, peeled and deveined
- 1/2 cup (115g) unsalted butter
- 3 garlic cloves, minced
- Zest and juice of 1 lemon
- 1/4 cup (60 g) fresh parsley, chopped
- Salt and freshly ground black pepper, to taste
- Red pepper flakes, optional, for a bit of heat

TOTAL NUTRITIONAL VALUE

Calories: 2,600; Protein: 90g; Carbohydrates: 290g;
Fat: 140g; Fiber: 2g; Sugar: 3g

DIRECTIONS

1. Prepare the dough using the listed ingredients and shape into fettuccine following the step-by-step Directions.
2. In a large skillet, melt the butter over medium heat. Add the minced garlic and sauté until fragrant.
3. Add the shrimp to the skillet and cook until they turn pink and are cooked through.
4. Stir in the lemon zest, lemon juice, and parsley. Season with salt, black pepper, and red pepper flakes if using.
5. Meanwhile, cook the fettuccine in a large pot of boiling salted water until al dente. Before draining the pasta, reserve about 1/2 cup (120 ml) of the cooking water.
6. Drain the fettuccine and add to the skillet with the shrimp and lemon butter sauce. If the sauce is too thick or if you desire a glossier sauce, gradually add the reserved cooking water until you reach the desired consistency.
7. Toss to combine and serve immediately.

PAPPARDELLE

Nestled in the culinary traditions of Tuscany and Umbria, pappardelle stands as a testament to the beauty of simplicity. With its wide, ribbon-like strands, it's a pasta that demands attention on the plate.

The name, inspired by the playful Italian verb "pappare," meaning "to gobble up," is a nod to its irresistible nature. Pappardelle's generous width is not just for show; it serves a purpose. It's designed to cradle and complement a myriad of sauces, from the rich and robust to the light and aromatic.

As you immerse yourself in the recipes that follow, you'll discover the versatility of pappardelle. Whether it's twirled around a fork with a classic tomato sauce or paired with a delicate infusion of herbs and olive oil, pappardelle promises a culinary experience that's both comforting and memorable.

As we journey through its history and variations, let's celebrate this pasta's unique ability to bring together ingredients in harmonious symphony, creating dishes that resonate with the heart and soul of Italian cooking.

Step-by-Step Guide:

SERVING: 4-6 people

INGREDIENTS:

- 400 g "Tipo 00" Flour or all-purpose flour
- 228 g Eggs – about four medium eggs

DIRECTIONS:

1. **Mixing the Dough:**
   - On a large, clean work surface or in a large bowl, pour flour into a mound. Create a well in the center that's about 4 inches wide.
   - Gently whisk the eggs using a fork, slowly incorporating the flour from the edges. As the mixture starts coming together, use your hands to fold in the remaining flour until a dough forms.
   - The dough should be firm but not too dry. If it's too sticky, add a sprinkle of flour. If it's too dry and crumbly, you can add a few drops of water.

2. **Kneading:**
   - Press the dough together to form a cohesive ball.
   - Place the dough on a floured surface. Use the heel of your hand to push the dough away from you, then fold it back over itself. Give the dough a quarter turn and repeat for about 8-10 minutes until the dough is smooth and elastic.
   - Once kneaded, shape the dough into a ball and let it rest covered tightly with plastic wrap for at least 30 minutes.

3. **Rolling the Dough:**
   - Divide your dough into manageable pieces, about the size of a lemon and pre-shape it into a rough oval shape.
   - Start at the widest setting on your pasta machine.
   - Feed the dough through the rollers. After the first pass, fold the dough in half or into thirds and pass it through the widest setting again.
   - Gradually reduce the roller setting, passing the dough through each time until you reach the desired thickness.

4. **Shaping the Pappardelle:**
   - Set your pasta maker to setting 6 or 7 if you're using a Mercato Atlas, or to setting 5 or 6 if you're using a KitchenAid attachment.
   - Roll the dough through the machine a couple of times to achieve the desired thickness.
   - Place the rolled dough on a floured surface and leave to dry for 10-15 minutes.
   - Pasta Cutter: Utilize either a straight or serrated pasta cutter to cut the dough sheets into ribbons approximately 2,5cm to 3cm wide. For straight lines and uniformity, you may use a ruler if you wish.
   - Sharp Knife: Begin by folding the dough sheets from the shorter sides to form a loose log. Using a sharp knife, cut this dough roll into strands around 2,5cm to 3cm in width.
   - Collect the pappardelle in a bowl with a bit of flour, gently tossing to prevent sticking.
   - Lay the finished pappardelle on a dry tea towel.

PAPPARDELLE WITH BLACK SQUID INK AND SCALLOPS

SERVES:4-6   PREP: 40 min   COOK: 25 min

INGREDIENTS

For the Dough:
- 280g "Tipo 00" Flour or all-purpose flour
- 2 whole large eggs (114g)
- 4 yolks from 4 large eggs (72g)
- 4 teaspoons squid ink (about 17g)

For the Seasoning:
- 1 lb (about 450g) fresh scallops
- 3 garlic cloves, minced
- 1/4 cup (60 ml) white wine
- 1/4 cup (60 ml) extra virgin olive oil
- Salt and freshly ground black pepper, to taste
- Fresh parsley, chopped, for garnish
- Lemon zest, for garnish

DIRECTIONS

1. Prepare the dough using the listed ingredients and shape into pappardelle following the step-by-step Directions.
2. In a large skillet, heat olive oil over medium-high heat. Add the minced garlic and sauté until fragrant.
3. Add the scallops to the skillet, ensuring they are not overcrowded. Sear each side for about 1-2 minutes or until a golden crust forms.
4. Pour in the white wine and let it simmer for 2 minutes, allowing the alcohol to evaporate.
5. Meanwhile, cook the black squid ink pappardelle in a large pot of boiling salted water until al dente. Drain and add to the skillet with the scallops.
6. Toss the pasta well to coat with the scallop mixture. Season with salt and pepper. Serve garnished with chopped fresh parsley and lemon zest.

TOTAL NUTRITIONAL VALUE

Calories: 2,300; Protein: 120g; Carbohydrates: 280g; Fat: 70g; Fiber: 5g; Sugar: 5g

PAPPARDELLE WITH SLOW-COOKED BEEF RAGU

SERVES:4-6   PREP: 30 min   COOK: 3 hours

INGREDIENTS

For the Dough:
- 400g "Tipo 00" Flour or all-purpose flour
- 228g Eggs – about four medium eggs

For the Seasoning:
- 1 lb (about 450g) beef chuck or stew meat, cut into chunks
- 1 onion, finely chopped
- 2 carrots, finely chopped
- 2 celery stalks, finely chopped
- 3 garlic cloves, minced
- 1 cup (240 ml) red wine
- 1 can (28 oz or 800g) crushed tomatoes
- 1/4 cup (60 ml) beef broth or stock
- 2 bay leaves
- Salt and freshly ground black pepper, to taste
- Grated Parmesan cheese, for serving

DIRECTIONS

1. Prepare the dough using the listed ingredients and shape into pappardelle following the step-by-step Directions.
2. In a large pot or Dutch oven, heat olive oil over medium heat. Brown the beef chunks on all sides and set aside.
3. In the same pot, add the onions, carrots, celery, and garlic. Sauté until the vegetables are softened.
4. Return the beef to the pot and pour in the red wine. Let it simmer until reduced by half.
5. Add the crushed tomatoes, beef broth, and bay leaves. Season with salt and pepper. Reduce the heat to low, cover, and let it simmer for 2.5 hours, stirring occasionally.
6. After the beef is tender, shred it in the sauce using two forks.
7. Cook the pappardelle in a large pot of boiling salted water until al dente. Drain and add to the pot with the beef ragu.
8. Toss the pasta well to coat with the sauce. Serve with freshly grated Parmesan cheese on top.

TOTAL NUTRITIONAL VALUE

Calories: 2,800; Protein: 140g; Carbohydrates: 300g; Fat: 90g; Fiber: 20g; Sugar: 15g

SPINACH PAPPARDELLE WITH CREAMY TOMATO SAUCE

SERVES: 4-6 PREP: 35 min COOK: 30 min

INGREDIENTS

For the Dough:
- 280g "Tipo 00" Flour or all-purpose flour
- 5 yolks from 5 large eggs (90g)
- 1 whole large egg (57g)
- 56g spinach purée

For the Seasoning:
- 1 can (28 oz or 800g) crushed tomatoes
- 1/2 cup (120 ml) heavy cream
- 2 garlic cloves, minced
- 1/4 cup (60 ml) extra virgin olive oil
- Salt and freshly ground black pepper, to taste
- Fresh basil leaves, for garnish
- Grated Parmesan cheese, for serving

DIRECTIONS

1. Prepare the dough using the listed ingredients and shape into pappardelle following the step-by-step Directions.
2. In a large skillet, heat olive oil over medium heat. Add the minced garlic and sauté until fragrant.
3. Pour in the crushed tomatoes and let it simmer for 20 minutes.
4. Stir in the heavy cream and continue to simmer for another 5 minutes. Season with salt and pepper.
5. Meanwhile, cook the spinach pappardelle in a large pot of boiling salted water until al dente. Before draining the pasta, reserve about 1/2 cup (120 ml) of the cooking water.
6. Drain the pappardelle and add to the skillet with the creamy tomato sauce. If the sauce is too thick or if you desire a creamier consistency, gradually add the reserved cooking water until you reach the desired consistency.
7. Serve garnished with fresh basil leaves and grated Parmesan cheese.

TOTAL NUTRITIONAL VALUE

Calories: 2,400; Protein: 80g; Carbohydrates: 280g; Fat: 110g; Fiber: 10g; Sugar: 12g

BEET PAPPARDELLE WITH GOAT CHEESE AND ARUGULA

SERVES: 4-6 PREP: 40 min COOK: 25 min

INGREDIENTS

For the Dough:
- 280g "Tipo 00" Flour or all-purpose flour
- 5 yolks from 5 large eggs (90g)
- 1 whole large egg (57g)
- 56g beet purée

For the Seasoning:
- 1 cup (150g) fresh arugula
- 1/2 cup (100g) goat cheese, crumbled
- 1/4 cup (60 ml) extra virgin olive oil
- Salt and freshly ground black pepper, to taste
- Lemon zest, for garnish (optional)

DIRECTIONS

1. Prepare the dough using the listed ingredients and shape into pappardelle following the step-by-step Directions.
2. In a large skillet, heat the olive oil over medium heat. Add the crumbled goat cheese, allowing it to melt slightly and create a creamy base.
3. Add the arugula to the skillet, stirring until it just begins to wilt.
4. Cook the purple-red beet pappardelle in a large pot of boiling salted water until al dente. Drain and add to the skillet with the goat cheese and arugula mixture.
5. Toss the pasta well to combine, ensuring it's coated with the creamy goat cheese sauce. Season with salt and pepper. Serve with a sprinkle of lemon zest (if using).

TOTAL NUTRITIONAL VALUE

Calories: 2,200; Protein: 70g; Carbohydrates: 260g; Fat: 90g; Fiber: 8g; Sugar: 10g

PAPPARDELLE WITH WILD MUSHROOMS AND PARMESAN

SERVES: 4-6   PREP: 20 min   COOK: 30 min

INGREDIENTS

For the Dough:
- 400g "Tipo 00" Flour or all-purpose flour
- 228g Eggs – about four medium eggs

For the Seasoning:
- 2 cups (about 300g) mixed wild mushrooms (e.g., shiitake, oyster, chanterelle), cleaned and sliced
- 3 garlic cloves, minced
- 1/4 cup (60 ml) extra virgin olive oil
- 1/2 cup (120 ml) white wine
- Salt and freshly ground black pepper, to taste
- 1/2 cup (50g) freshly grated Parmesan cheese
- Fresh parsley, chopped, for garnish

DIRECTIONS

1. Prepare the dough using the listed ingredients and shape into pappardelle following the step-by-step Directions.
2. In a large skillet, heat olive oil over medium heat. Add the minced garlic and sauté until fragrant.
3. Add the sliced wild mushrooms to the skillet and cook until they release their moisture and become tender.
4. Pour in the white wine and let it simmer until reduced by half.
5. Meanwhile, cook the pappardelle in a large pot of boiling salted water until al dente. Before draining the pasta, reserve about 1/2 cup (120 ml) of the cooking water.
6. Drain the pappardelle and add to the skillet with the mushroom mixture.
7. Toss the pasta well to combine with the mushrooms. If the mixture is too dry or if you desire a glossier sauce, gradually add the reserved cooking water until you reach the desired consistency.
8. Season with salt and pepper. Serve topped with freshly grated Parmesan cheese and garnished with chopped parsley.

TOTAL NUTRITIONAL VALUE

Calories: 2,500; Protein: 90g; Carbohydrates: 290g; Fat: 100g; Fiber: 8g; Sugar: 6g

PAPPARDELLE WITH ROASTED CHICKEN AND ROSEMARY

SERVES: 4-6   PREP: 20 min   COOK: 40 min

INGREDIENTS

For the Dough:
- 400g "Tipo 00" Flour or all-purpose flour
- 228g Eggs – about four medium eggs

For the Seasoning:
- 2 chicken breasts, roasted and shredded
- 2 sprigs fresh rosemary, leaves removed and finely chopped
- 3 garlic cloves, minced
- 1/4 cup (60 ml) extra virgin olive oil
- 1/2 cup (120 ml) chicken broth or stock
- Salt and freshly ground black pepper, to taste
- Grated Parmesan cheese, for serving

DIRECTIONS

1. Prepare the dough using the listed ingredients and shape into pappardelle following the step-by-step Directions.
2. In a large skillet, heat olive oil over medium heat. Add the minced garlic and chopped rosemary, sautéing until fragrant.
3. Add the shredded roasted chicken to the skillet and stir to combine.
4. Pour in the chicken broth and let it simmer for a few minutes to meld the flavors.
5. Meanwhile, cook the pappardelle in a large pot of boiling salted water until al dente.
6. Before draining the pasta, reserve about 1/2 cup (120 ml) of the cooking water.
7. Drain the pappardelle and add to the skillet with the chicken and rosemary mixture.
8. Toss the pasta well to combine. If the mixture is too dry or if you desire a glossier sauce, gradually add the reserved cooking water until you reach the desired consistency.
9. Season with salt and pepper. Serve with freshly grated Parmesan cheese on top.

TOTAL NUTRITIONAL VALUE

Calories: 2,400; Protein: 110g; Carbohydrates: 280g; Fat: 90g; Fiber: 6g; Sugar: 5g

PAPPARDELLE WITH BACON AND PEAS IN CREAM SAUCE

SERVES: 4-6   PREP: 20 min   COOK: 30 min

INGREDIENTS

For the Dough:
- 400g "Tipo 00" Flour or all-purpose flour
- 228g Eggs – about four medium eggs

For the Seasoning:
- 6 strips of bacon, chopped
- 1 cup (150g) fresh or frozen peas
- 2 garlic cloves, minced
- 1 cup (240 ml) heavy cream
- Salt and freshly ground black pepper, to taste
- Grated Parmesan cheese, for serving
- Fresh parsley, chopped, for garnish

TOTAL NUTRITIONAL VALUE

Calories: 2,600; Protein: 80g; Carbohydrates: 290g; Fat: 140g; Fiber: 6g; Sugar: 8g

DIRECTIONS

1. Prepare the dough using the listed ingredients and shape into pappardelle following the step-by-step Directions.
2. In a large skillet, cook the chopped bacon over medium heat until crispy. Remove the bacon and set aside, leaving the rendered fat in the skillet.
3. Add the minced garlic to the skillet and sauté until fragrant.
4. Pour in the heavy cream and let it simmer for a few minutes.
5. Add the peas to the skillet and cook until they are tender (if using fresh peas) or heated through (if using frozen peas).
6. Meanwhile, cook the pappardelle in a large pot of boiling salted water until al dente. Before draining the pasta, reserve about 1/2 cup (120 ml) of the cooking water.
7. Drain the pappardelle and add to the skillet with the cream and pea mixture.
8. Add the crispy bacon back to the skillet and toss the pasta well to combine. If the mixture is too dry or if you desire a glossier sauce, gradually add the reserved cooking water until you reach the desired consistency.
9. Season with salt and pepper. Serve topped with freshly grated Parmesan cheese and garnished with chopped parsley.

PAPPARDELLE WITH SPINACH AND RICOTTA

SERVES: 4-6   PREP: 20 min   COOK: 25 min

INGREDIENTS

For the Dough:
- 400g "Tipo 00" Flour or all-purpose flour
- 228g Eggs – about four medium eggs

For the Seasoning:
- 2 cups (about 60g) fresh spinach, washed and roughly chopped
- 1 cup (250g) ricotta cheese
- 2 garlic cloves, minced
- 1/4 cup (60 ml) extra virgin olive oil
- Salt and freshly ground black pepper, to taste
- Grated Parmesan cheese, for serving
- Fresh basil leaves, for garnish

TOTAL NUTRITIONAL VALUE

Calories: 2,300; Protein: 90g; Carbohydrates: 280g; Fat: 100g; Fiber: 6g; Sugar: 5g

DIRECTIONS

1. Prepare the dough using the listed ingredients and shape into pappardelle following the step-by-step Directions.
2. In a large skillet, heat olive oil over medium heat. Add the minced garlic and sauté until fragrant.
3. Add the chopped spinach to the skillet and cook until wilted.
4. Reduce the heat to low and stir in the ricotta cheese, mixing until smooth and creamy.
5. Meanwhile, cook the pappardelle in a large pot of boiling salted water until al dente. Before draining the pasta, reserve about 1/2 cup (120 ml) of the cooking water.
6. Drain the pappardelle and add to the skillet with the spinach and ricotta mixture.
7. Toss the pasta well to combine with the sauce. If the mixture is too dry or if you desire a glossier sauce, gradually add the reserved cooking water until you reach the desired consistency.
8. Season with salt and pepper. Serve topped with freshly grated Parmesan cheese and garnished with fresh basil leaves.

PAPPARDELLE WITH BUTTERNUT SQUASH AND SAGE BROWN BUTTER

SERVES: 4-6 PREP: 25 min COOK: 35 min

INGREDIENTS

For the Dough:
- 400g "Tipo 00" Flour or all-purpose flour
- 228g Eggs – about four medium eggs

For the Seasoning:
- 2 cups (about 300g) butternut squash, peeled and diced
- 6 fresh sage leaves
- 1/2 cup (115g) unsalted butter
- 2 garlic cloves, minced
- Salt and freshly ground black pepper, to taste
- Grated Parmesan cheese, for serving
- Toasted pine nuts, for garnish (optional)

DIRECTIONS

1. Prepare the dough using the listed ingredients and shape into pappardelle following the step-by-step Directions.
2. In a large skillet, melt the butter over medium heat. Continue to cook until the butter starts to brown and has a nutty aroma.
3. Add the sage leaves to the skillet and let them crisp up in the browned butter.
4. Add the minced garlic and diced butternut squash. Cook until the squash is tender and slightly caramelized.
5. Meanwhile, cook the pappardelle in a large pot of boiling salted water until al dente. Drain and add to the skillet with the butternut squash mixture.
6. Toss the pasta well to combine with the sage brown butter sauce. Season with salt and pepper. Serve topped with freshly grated Parmesan cheese and garnished with toasted pine nuts, if desired.

TOTAL NUTRITIONAL VALUE

Calories: 2,500; Protein: 70g; Carbohydrates: 290g;
Fat: 130g; Fiber: 6g; Sugar: 8g;

TOMATO PAPPARDELLE WITH ANCHOVIES, CHERRY TOMATOES, AND OLIVES

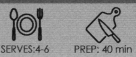

SERVES: 4-6 PREP: 40 min COOK: 25 min

INGREDIENTS

For the Dough:
- 280g "Tipo 00" Flour or all-purpose flour
- 5 yolks from 5 large eggs (90g)
- 1 whole large egg (57g)
- 56g tomato paste

For the Seasoning:
- 1 can (2 oz or 56g) anchovy fillets, drained and chopped
- 1 cup (150g) cherry tomatoes, halved
- 1/2 cup (90g) black olives, pitted and sliced
- 3 garlic cloves, minced
- 1/4 cup (60 ml) extra virgin olive oil
- Salt and freshly ground black pepper, to taste
- Fresh parsley, chopped, for garnish

DIRECTIONS

1. Prepare the dough using the listed ingredients and shape into pappardelle following the step-by-step Directions.
2. In a large skillet, heat olive oil over medium heat. Add the minced garlic and sauté until fragrant.
3. Add the chopped anchovies to the skillet and cook until they melt into the oil.
4. Stir in the halved cherry tomatoes and sliced olives, cooking until the tomatoes are slightly softened.
5. Meanwhile, cook the orange tomato pappardelle in a large pot of boiling salted water until al dente. Drain and add to the skillet with the anchovy and tomato mixture.
6. Toss the pasta well to combine. Season with salt and pepper. Serve garnished with chopped fresh parsley.

TOTAL NUTRITIONAL VALUE

Calories: 2,300; Protein: 80g; Carbohydrates: 280g;
Fat: 90g; Fiber: 7g; Sugar: 9g

LASAGNE

Ah, lasagne! A dish that has woven its way into the fabric of Italian culinary history and has been embraced with open arms by families across the globe. Originating from the ancient Greek word "laganon," which referred to a flat sheet of pasta dough, lasagne has evolved over the centuries, finding its true essence in the heart of Italy, especially in regions like Emilia-Romagna. Here, layers of pasta are meticulously assembled with rich sauces, cheeses, and sometimes meats or vegetables, creating a symphony of flavors in every bite.

Now, my dear ones, as we delve into this chapter dedicated to lasagne recipes, I want to ensure you have all the tools and knowledge at your fingertips. From the traditional lasagne alla Bolognese to innovative vegetarian delights, each recipe tells a story, and I'm eager to share these with you. But before we dive into these mouth-watering recipes, it's essential to master the basics.

You might remember our earlier discussion on crafting the perfect lasagne noodles. We'll be revisiting that process, ensuring you have a clear understanding of every step. And, of course, I haven't forgotten the most anticipated part - assembling these layers to perfection. It felt only right to include this essential information right here, at the beginning of our lasagne adventure. After all, understanding the foundation will only enhance the joy of exploring the recipes that follow.

So, gather around the kitchen table, and let's embark on this delightful culinary journey, where we'll weave together layers of tradition, innovation, and love.

Step-by-Step Guide:

SERVING: 6-8 people

INGREDIENTS:

- 300 g "Tipo 00" Flour or all-purpose flour
- 171 g Eggs – about 3 medium eggs

DIRECTIONS:

1. **Mixing the Dough:**
   - On a large, clean work surface or in a large bowl, pour flour into a mound. Create a well in the center that's about 4 inches wide.
   - Gently whisk the eggs using a fork, slowly incorporating the flour from the edges. As the mixture starts coming together, use your hands to fold in the remaining flour until a dough forms.
   - The dough should be firm but not too dry. If it's too sticky, add a sprinkle of flour. If it's too dry and crumbly, you can add a few drops of water.

2. **Kneading:**
   - Press the dough together to form a cohesive ball.
   - Place the dough on a floured surface. Use the heel of your hand to push the dough away from you, then fold it back over itself. Give the dough a quarter turn and repeat for about 8-10 minutes until the dough is smooth and elastic.
   - Once kneaded, shape the dough into a ball and let it rest covered tightly with plastic wrap for at least 30 minutes.

3. **Rolling the Dough:**
   - Divide your dough into manageable pieces, about the size of a lemon and pre-shape it into a rough oval shape.
   - Start at the widest setting on your pasta machine.
   - Feed the dough through the rollers. After the first pass, fold the dough in half or into thirds and pass it through the widest setting again.
   - Gradually reduce the roller setting, passing the dough through each time until you reach the desired thickness.

4. **Shaping the Lasagne:**
   - Set your pasta maker to setting 6 if you're using a Mercato Atlas 150, or to setting 4 or 5 if you're using a KitchenAid attachment.
   - Roll the dough through the machine a couple of times to achieve the desired thickness.
   - Cut the pasta sheets to fit the dimensions of the baking dish you'll be using to assemble the lasagna. For example, using a 9x13" baking pan, with the quantities in this recipe, you should get 10-12 lasagna noodles about the size of 5x12" each.
   - Lay the lasagna noodles, obtained from the first ball of dough, in a single layer on a baking sheet lined with parchment paper. Cover with another sheet of parchment paper to prevent them from drying out.
   - Repeat the process with the remaining three pieces of dough.

5. Assembling the Lasagne:

- Begin by spreading a thin layer of your chosen sauce at the bottom of your baking dish. This prevents the noodles from sticking and creates a flavorful base.
- Place a layer of lasagna noodles over the sauce, ensuring they slightly overlap.
- Add a layer of your filling, whether it's meat, cheese, vegetables, or a combination.
- Continue layering in this order: sauce, noodles, filling, until you've used up all your ingredients. Finish with a final layer of sauce and a generous sprinkle of cheese on top.
- Cover the baking dish with aluminum foil and bake in a preheated oven. Once baked, let it rest for at least 15 minutes to allow the flavors to meld and the lasagna to set.

Note: The exact baking time and temperature will vary based on the specific lasagna recipe you're following. Always refer to the individual recipe for precise Directions.

Do I Need to Pre-Cook the Lasagna Noodles?

Ah, the age-old debate in many Italian-American households: to pre-cook or not to pre-cook the lasagna noodles? Well, dear ones, let me share a bit of wisdom from my years in the kitchen. The choice truly hinges on the type of filling you're using for your lasagna.

Imagine you're preparing a lasagna that's brimming with a rich, saucy filling. In such cases, there's no need to pre-cook those noodles. The abundant moisture from that luscious sauce will lovingly cook the noodles as everything bakes together in the oven..

However, if you're leaning towards a lasagna with a filling that's a tad on the drier side, or perhaps you've let your lasagna noodles dry out a bit more than usual, then it's a good idea to give them a quick dip in boiling water. This ensures that when you pull that lasagna out of the oven, each layer is perfectly soft and melds beautifully with the filling.

Tips for Pre-Cooking Lasagna Noodles:

1. **Boiling:** Gently place a couple of lasagna noodles into a pot of boiling, salted water. Allow them to par-boil for about 30 seconds.
2. **Rinsing:** After boiling, immediately transfer the noodles to a colander using a slotted spoon. Rinse them under cold water. This step is crucial as it washes off excess starch (preventing the noodles from sticking together) and stops the cooking process.
3. **Drying:** Lay the rinsed noodles on clean kitchen towels, ensuring they're separated. This helps them dry without sticking to each other. You can use them right away or store them in an airtight container, with layers separated by parchment paper, for later use.

Béchamel Sauce:

Before we dive into the world of lasagna recipe, there's a foundational sauce that deserves our attention: the béchamel sauce. Often referred to as "white sauce," béchamel is a creamy, velvety sauce that adds richness and depth to many lasagna recipes. It's the glue that binds our layers together, providing moisture and a luscious mouthfeel.

Whether you're crafting a traditional lasagna alla Bolognese or experimenting with unique fillings, a well-made béchamel can elevate your dish to new heights. Let's learn how to make this essential component:

SERVING: About 4 cups (1 liter)

INGREDIENTS:

- 4 cups (1 liter) whole milk
- 4 tbsp (60g) unsalted butter
- 6 tbsp (45g) all-purpose flour
- 1/4 tsp freshly grated nutmeg
- Salt and white pepper, to taste

DIRECTIONS.

1. In a saucepan, heat the milk until it's just about to boil, then remove from heat.
2. In a separate, larger saucepan, melt the butter over medium heat. Once melted, add the flour, whisking continuously to create a smooth roux. Cook the roux for 2 minutes, ensuring it doesn't brown.
3. Gradually add the warmed milk to the roux, whisking continuously to prevent lumps from forming.
4. Continue to cook and whisk the mixture until it thickens to the consistency of heavy cream, which usually takes about 8-10 minutes.
5. Remove from heat and season with nutmeg, salt, and white pepper. If not using immediately, cover the surface with plastic wrap to prevent a skin from forming.

CLASSIC LASAGNA ALLA BOLOGNESE

SERVES: 6-8 PREP: 45 min COOK: 50 min

INGREDIENTS

For the Dough:
- 300g "Tipo 00" Flour or all-purpose flour
- 171g Eggs – about 3 medium eggs

For the Béchamel:
- 4 cups (1 liter) whole milk
- 4 tbsp (60g) unsalted butter
- 6 tbsp (45g) all-purpose flour
- 1/4 tsp freshly grated nutmeg
- Salt and white pepper, to taste

For the Seasoning:
- 1 lb (450g) ground beef
- 1 lb (450g) ground pork
- 1 large onion, finely chopped
- 2 garlic cloves, minced
- 1 can (28 oz) crushed tomatoes
- 1/4 cup (60ml) red wine (optional)
- 2 tbsp olive oil
- Salt and pepper, to taste
- 2 cups béchamel sauce
- 1 cup (100g) grated Parmesan cheese

TOTAL NUTRITIONAL VALUE

Calories: 4,800; Protein: 280g; Carbohydrates: 320g; Fat: 260g; Fiber: 16g; Sugar: 24g

DIRECTIONS

1. Prepare the dough using the listed ingredients and shape into lasagna noodles following the step-by-step Directions. Given the rich and saucy nature of the Bolognese, there's no need to pre-cook the noodles.
2. Prepare the béchamel sauce following the Directions. given above
3. In a large skillet, heat olive oil over medium heat. Add onions and garlic, sautéing until translucent. Add the ground beef and pork, cooking until browned. Drain excess fat.
4. Pour in the crushed tomatoes and red wine (if using). Season with salt and pepper. Let it simmer for 20-25 minutes.
5. Preheat your oven to 375°F (190°C).
6. Assemble the lasagna in a 9x13" baking dish by spreading a thin layer of meat sauce at the bottom. Place a layer of lasagna noodles over the sauce. Spread a layer of béchamel sauce over the noodles, followed by a sprinkle of Parmesan cheese. Repeat layers until all ingredients are used, finishing with a layer of meat sauce and a generous sprinkle of Parmesan on top.
7. Cover with aluminum foil and bake for 30 minutes. Remove foil and bake for an additional 20 minutes, or until bubbly and golden.
8. Let it rest for at least 15 minutes before serving.

WHITE LASAGNA WITH CHICKEN AND SPINACH

SERVES: 6-8 PREP: 40 min COOK: 50 min

INGREDIENTS

For the Dough:
- 300g "Tipo 00" Flour or all-purpose flour
- 171g Eggs – about 3 medium eggs

For the Seasoning:
- 1 lb (450g) boneless, skinless chicken breasts, cooked and shredded
- 2 cups fresh spinach, roughly chopped
- 4 cups béchamel sauce
- 1 cup (100g) grated Parmesan cheese
- 2 cups (200g) shredded mozzarella cheese
- 2 tbsp olive oil
- 2 garlic cloves, minced
- Salt and pepper, to taste

TOTAL NUTRITIONAL VALUE

Calories: 4,500; Protein: 310g; Carbohydrates: 310g; Fat: 230g; Fiber: 8g; Sugar: 20g;

DIRECTIONS

1. Prepare the dough using the listed ingredients and shape into lasagna noodles following the step-by-step Directions. Since the filling is creamy but not overly juicy, consider pre-cooking the lasagna noodles following the Directions. given above.
2. In a skillet, heat olive oil over medium heat. Add garlic and sauté until fragrant. Add the chopped spinach and cook until wilted. Season with salt and pepper. Remove from heat and mix in the shredded chicken.
3. Preheat your oven to 375°F (190°C).
4. Assemble the lasagna in a 9x13" baking dish by spreading a thin layer of béchamel sauce at the bottom. Place a layer of lasagna noodles over the sauce. Spread a layer of the chicken and spinach mixture, followed by a sprinkle of both Parmesan and mozzarella cheeses. Repeat layers until all ingredients are used, finishing with a layer of béchamel sauce and a generous sprinkle of both cheeses on top.
5. Cover with aluminum foil and bake for 30 minutes. Remove foil and bake for an additional 20 minutes, or until bubbly and golden.
6. Let it rest for at least 15 minutes before serving.

NOTE

When cooking the spinach, ensure you drain any excess liquid after sautéing to prevent the lasagna from becoming too watery. If using store-bought rotisserie chicken, be mindful of its salt content and adjust the seasoning of the filling accordingly.

VEGETARIAN LASAGNA WiTH ROASTED VEGETABLES

SERVES:6-8   PREP: 50 min   COOK: 55 min

INGREDIENTS

For the Dough:
- 300g "Tipo 00" Flour or all-purpose flour
- 171g Eggs – about 3 medium eggs

For the Seasoning:
- 1 zucchini, sliced
- 1 bell pepper, sliced
- 1 eggplant, sliced
- 2 cups ricotta cheese
- 1 cup (100g) grated mozzarella cheese
- 1/4 cup (25g) grated Parmesan cheese
- 2 cups tomato sauce
- 2 tbsp olive oil
- Salt and pepper, to taste

TOTAL NUTRITIONAL VALUE

Calories: 4,200; Protein: 240g; Carbohydrates: 300g; Fat: 220g; Fiber: 20g; Sugar: 28g

DIRECTIONS

1. Prepare the dough using the listed ingredients and shape into lasagna noodles following the step-by-step Directions. Given the drier nature of roasted vegetables, consider pre-cooking the lasagna noodles following the Directions. given above.
2. Preheat your oven to 400°F (200°C). Toss the sliced vegetables in olive oil, salt, and pepper. Spread them out on a baking sheet and roast for 20-25 minutes or until tender and slightly caramelized.
3. Reduce the oven temperature to 375°F (190°C).
4. Assemble the lasagna in a 9x13" baking dish by spreading a thin layer of tomato sauce at the bottom. Place a layer of lasagna noodles over the sauce. Spread a layer of ricotta cheese, followed by the roasted vegetables, and then a sprinkle of mozzarella and Parmesan cheeses. Repeat layers until all ingredients are used, finishing with a layer of tomato sauce and a generous sprinkle of both cheeses on top.
5. Cover with aluminum foil and bake for 30 minutes. Remove foil and bake for an additional 25 minutes, or until bubbly and golden.
6. Let it rest for at least 15 minutes before serving.

WHiTE MUSHROOM LASAGNA

SERVES:6-8   PREP: 40 min   COOK: 50 min

INGREDIENTS

For the Dough:
- 300g "Tipo 00" Flour or all-purpose flour
- 171g Eggs – about 3 medium eggs

For the Béchamel:
- 4 cups (1 liter) whole milk
- 4 tbsp (60g) unsalted butter
- 6 tbsp (45g) all-purpose flour
- 1/4 tsp freshly grated nutmeg
- Salt and white pepper, to taste

For the Seasoning:
- 1 lb (450g) mixed mushrooms (like cremini, shiitake, and portobello), sliced
- 4 cups béchamel sauce
- 1 cup (100g) grated Parmesan cheese
- 2 cups (200g) shredded mozzarella cheese
- 2 tbsp olive oil
- 2 garlic cloves, minced
- 2 tsp fresh thyme, chopped
- Salt and pepper, to taste

TOTAL NUTRITIONAL VALUE

Calories: 4,600; Protein: 260g; Carbohydrates: 310g; Fat: 250g; Fiber: 18g; Sugar: 22g

DIRECTIONS

1. Prepare the dough using the listed ingredients and shape into lasagna noodles following the step-by-step Directions. Given the creamy nature of the béchamel sauce, there's no need to pre-cook the noodles.
2. Prepare the béchamel sauce following the Directions. given above.
3. In a skillet, heat olive oil over medium heat. Add garlic and sauté until fragrant. Add the sliced mushrooms and thyme, cooking until the mushrooms release their moisture and become golden brown. Season with salt and pepper.
4. Preheat your oven to 375°F (190°C).
5. Assemble the lasagna in a 9x13" baking dish by spreading a thin layer of béchamel sauce at the bottom. Place a layer of lasagna noodles over the sauce. Spread a layer of the mushroom mixture, followed by a sprinkle of both Parmesan and mozzarella cheeses. Repeat layers until all ingredients are used, finishing with a layer of béchamel sauce and a generous sprinkle of both cheeses on top.
6. Cover with aluminum foil and bake for 30 minutes. Remove foil and bake for an additional 20 minutes, or until bubbly and golden.
7. Let it rest for at least 15 minutes before serving.

NOTE

If you find the mushroom mixture too dry, you can add a splash of white wine or vegetable broth while sautéing for added moisture and flavor.

SEAFOOD LASAGNA

SERVES:6-8   PREP: 40 min   COOK: 50 min

INGREDIENTS

For the Dough:
- 300g "Tipo 00" Flour or all-purpose flour
- 171g Eggs – about 3 medium eggs

For the Seasoning:
- 1 lb (450g) Shrimp, peeled and deveined
- 1 lb (450g) Scallops
- 1 lb (450g) Crabmeat
- 1 Onion, finely chopped
- 3 cloves Garlic, minced
- 1/4 cup (60ml) White Wine
- 2 cups (475ml) Tomato Sauce
- 1/4 cup (60ml) Heavy Cream
- 2 tbsp Olive Oil
- Salt and Pepper, to taste
- 2 cups (200g) Mozzarella Cheese, shredded
- 1/2 cup (50g) Parmesan Cheese, grated
- Fresh Parsley, chopped for garnish

TOTAL NUTRITIONAL VALUE

Calories: 4,200; Protein: 280g; Carbohydrates: 240g; Fat: 200g; Fiber: 12g; Sugar: 20g

DIRECTIONS

1. Prepare the dough using the listed ingredients and shape into lasagne noodles following the step-by-step Directions. Given the moisture content from the seafood and the béchamel sauce, there's no need to pre-cook the lasagna noodles. The abundant moisture will cook the noodles as everything bakes together in the oven.
2. In a large skillet, heat olive oil over medium heat. Add onions and garlic and sauté until translucent.
3. Add shrimp, scallops, and crabmeat to the skillet. Cook until the seafood is almost done, then pour in the white wine and let it reduce by half.
4. Stir in the tomato sauce and heavy cream. Season with salt and pepper. Let the sauce simmer for 10 minutes.
5. Preheat your oven to 375°F (190°C).
6. Begin assembling the lasagna by spreading a thin layer of the seafood sauce at the bottom of a 9x13" baking dish. Place a layer of lasagna noodles over the sauce. Spread another layer of seafood sauce, then sprinkle with mozzarella and Parmesan cheese.
7. Continue layering in this order: noodles, sauce, cheeses, until you've used up all your ingredients. Finish with a final layer of sauce and a generous sprinkle of cheese on top.
8. Cover the baking dish with aluminum foil and bake in the preheated oven for 30 minutes. Remove the foil and bake for an additional 10 minutes, or until the cheese is bubbly and golden.
9. Let the lasagna rest for at least 15 minutes before serving. Garnish with fresh parsley.

THREE-CHEESE LASAGNA

SERVES:6-8   PREP: 30 min   COOK: 45 min

INGREDIENTS

For the Dough:
- 300g "Tipo 00" Flour or all-purpose flour
- 171g Eggs – about 3 medium eggs

For the Seasoning:
- 2 cups (475ml) Tomato Sauce
- 2 cups (475g) Ricotta Cheese
- 2 cups (200g) Mozzarella Cheese, shredded
- 1 cup (100g) Parmesan Cheese, grated
- 1 Egg
- 2 tbsp Fresh Basil, chopped
- 2 tbsp Fresh Parsley, chopped
- Salt and Pepper, to taste

TOTAL NUTRITIONAL VALUE

Calories: 3,800; Protein: 220g; Carbohydrates: 220g; Fat: 180g; Fiber: 8g; Sugar: 18g

DIRECTIONS

1. Prepare the dough using the listed ingredients and shape into lasagne noodles following the step-by-step Directions. The tomato sauce and the moisture from the cheeses should provide enough liquid to cook the noodles in the oven. Thus, there's no need to pre-cook the lasagna noodles.
2. In a mixing bowl, combine ricotta cheese, half of the mozzarella, half of the Parmesan, egg, basil, parsley, salt, and pepper. Mix until well combined.
3. Preheat your oven to 375°F (190°C).
4. Begin assembling the lasagna by spreading a thin layer of tomato sauce at the bottom of a 9x13" baking dish. Place a layer of lasagna noodles over the sauce. Spread a layer of the cheese mixture, then sprinkle with some mozzarella and Parmesan cheese.
5. Continue layering in this order: noodles, tomato sauce, cheese mixture, mozzarella, and Parmesan, until you've used up all your ingredients. Finish with a final layer of tomato sauce and a generous sprinkle of cheese on top.
6. Cover the baking dish with aluminum foil and bake in the preheated oven for 30 minutes. Remove the foil and bake for an additional 15 minutes, or until the cheese is bubbly and golden.
7. Let the lasagna rest for at least 15 minutes before serving.

LASAGNA WITH PESTO AND SUN-DRIED TOMATOES

SERVES: 6-8   PREP: 35 min   COOK: 50 min

INGREDIENTS

For the Dough:
- 300g "Tipo 00" Flour or all-purpose flour
- 171g Eggs – about 3 medium eggs

For the Seasoning:
- 2 cups (475ml) Basil Pesto
- 1 cup (150g) Sun-Dried Tomatoes, chopped
- 2 cups (475g) Ricotta Cheese
- 2 cups (200g) Mozzarella Cheese, shredded
- 1 cup (100g) Parmesan Cheese, grated
- 1 Egg
- Salt and Pepper, to taste

DIRECTIONS

1. Prepare the dough using the listed ingredients and shape into lasagne noodles following the step-by-step Directions. The béchamel and pesto provide a good amount of moisture. However, to ensure the noodles are perfectly cooked, consider pre-cooking the lasagna noodles following the Directions. given above.
2. In a mixing bowl, combine ricotta cheese, half of the mozzarella, half of the Parmesan, egg, salt, and pepper. Mix until well combined.
3. Preheat your oven to 375°F (190°C).
4. Begin assembling the lasagna by spreading a thin layer of pesto at the bottom of a 9x13" baking dish. Place a layer of lasagna noodles over the pesto. Spread a layer of the cheese mixture, sprinkle with sun-dried tomatoes, then add some mozzarella and Parmesan cheese.
5. Continue layering in this order: noodles, pesto, cheese mixture, sun-dried tomatoes, mozzarella, and Parmesan, until you've used up all your ingredients. Finish with a final layer of pesto and a generous sprinkle of cheese on top.
6. Cover the baking dish with aluminum foil and bake in the preheated oven for 30 minutes. Remove the foil and bake for an additional 15 minutes, or until the cheese is bubbly and golden.
7. Let the lasagna rest for at least 15 minutes before serving.

TOTAL NUTRITIONAL VALUE

Calories: 4,100; Protein: 230g; Carbohydrates: 250g; Fat: 240g; Fiber: 10g; Sugar: 20g

NOTE

Sun-dried tomatoes can be quite intense in flavor. If you prefer a milder taste, you can soak them in warm water for about 10 minutes before chopping. This will also make them softer and easier to layer.

MEDITERRANEAN LASAGNA

SERVES: 6-8   PREP: 40 min   COOK: 50 min

INGREDIENTS

For the Dough:
- 300g "Tipo 00" Flour or all-purpose flour
- 171g Eggs – about 3 medium eggs

For the Seasoning:
- 2 cups (475ml) Tomato and Herb Sauce
- 1 cup (150g) Grilled Eggplant, sliced
- 1 cup (150g) Artichoke Hearts, chopped
- 1/2 cup (75g) Black Olives, sliced
- 1 cup (200g) Feta Cheese, crumbled
- 2 cups (200g) Mozzarella Cheese, shredded
- 1/2 cup (50g) Parmesan Cheese, grated
- Fresh Basil, for garnish
- Salt and Pepper, to taste

DIRECTIONS

1. Prepare the dough using the listed ingredients and shape into lasagne noodles following the step-by-step Directions. Given the moisture from the roasted vegetables and the tomato and herb sauce, there's no need to pre-cook the lasagna noodles.
2. Preheat your oven to 375°F (190°C).
3. Begin assembling the lasagna by spreading a thin layer of tomato and herb sauce at the bottom of a 9x13" baking dish. Place a layer of lasagna noodles over the sauce. Add a layer of grilled eggplant, artichoke hearts, and olives. Sprinkle with feta, mozzarella, and Parmesan cheese.
4. Continue layering in this order: noodles, sauce, vegetables, cheeses, until you've used up all your ingredients. Finish with a final layer of sauce and a generous sprinkle of cheese on top.
5. Cover the baking dish with aluminum foil and bake in the preheated oven for 30 minutes. Remove the foil and bake for an additional 15 minutes, or until the cheese is bubbly and golden.
6. Let the lasagna rest for at least 15 minutes before serving. Garnish with fresh basil.

TOTAL NUTRITIONAL VALUE

Calories: 3,900; Protein: 220g; Carbohydrates: 230g; Fat: 210g; Fiber: 12g; Sugar: 18g

NOTE

If you're using marinated artichoke hearts, you might want to reduce the amount of salt in the recipe, as the marinade often contains salt. Adjust seasoning according to your preference.

SALMON AND ZUCCHINI LASAGNA

SERVES:6-8   PREP: 40 min   COOK: 50 min

INGREDIENTS

For the Dough:
- 300g "Tipo 00" Flour or all-purpose flour
- 171g Eggs – about 3 medium eggs

For the Seasoning:
- 2 cups (500ml) Creamy Dill Béchamel Sauce (prepare the béchamel sauce following the Directions. given above, then stir in 2 tbsp of chopped fresh dill)
- 2 cups (300g) Smoked Salmon, thinly sliced
- 2 cups (300g) Zucchini, thinly sliced
- 2 cups (200g) Mozzarella Cheese, shredded
- 1 cup (100g) Parmesan Cheese, grated
- Fresh Dill, for garnish
- Salt and Pepper, to taste

DIRECTIONS

1. Prepare the dough using the listed ingredients and shape into lasagne noodles following the step-by-step Directions. The creamy dill béchamel sauce and the moisture from the zucchini should be sufficient to cook the noodles. Thus, there's no need to pre-cook the lasagna noodles.
2. Preheat your oven to 375°F (190°C).
3. Begin assembling the lasagna by spreading a thin layer of creamy dill béchamel sauce at the bottom of a 9x13" baking dish. Place a layer of lasagne noodles over the sauce. Add a layer of smoked salmon and zucchini slices. Sprinkle with mozzarella and Parmesan cheese.
4. Continue layering in this order: noodles, béchamel sauce, salmon, zucchini, cheeses, until you've used up all your ingredients. Finish with a final layer of béchamel sauce and a generous sprinkle of cheese on top.
5. Cover the baking dish with aluminum foil and bake in the preheated oven for 30 minutes. Remove the foil and bake for an additional 15 minutes, or until the cheese is bubbly and golden.
6. Let the lasagna rest for at least 15 minutes before serving. Garnish with fresh dill.

TOTAL NUTRITIONAL VALUE

Calories: 4,200; Protein: 240g; Carbohydrates: 220g; Fat: 230g; Fiber: 6g; Sugar: 12g

NOTE

Smoked salmon can be salty, so be cautious when adding additional salt to the recipe. Adjust seasoning according to your preference.

BUFFALO CHICKEN LASAGNA

SERVES:6-8   PREP: 40 min   COOK: 55 min

INGREDIENTS

For the Dough:
- 300g "Tipo 00" Flour or all-purpose flour
- 171g Eggs – about 3 medium eggs

For the Seasoning:
- 3 cups (700ml) Buffalo Chicken Sauce (store-bought or homemade)
- 3 cups (450g) Cooked Chicken, shredded
- 1 cup (100g) Blue Cheese, crumbled
- 2 cups (200g) Mozzarella Cheese, shredded
- 1/2 cup (50g) Parmesan Cheese, grated
- 1 cup (100g) Celery, finely chopped
- 1/2 cup (120ml) Ranch Dressing
- Salt and Pepper, to taste

DIRECTIONS

1. Prepare the dough using the listed ingredients and shape into lasagne noodles following the step-by-step Directions. The buffalo chicken sauce and ranch dressing provide a good amount of moisture. However, to ensure the noodles are perfectly cooked, consider pre-cooking the lasagna noodles following the Directions. given above.
2. Preheat your oven to 375°F (190°C).
3. Begin assembling the lasagna by spreading a thin layer of buffalo chicken sauce at the bottom of a 9x13" baking dish. Place a layer of lasagne noodles over the sauce. Add a layer of shredded chicken, drizzle with some ranch dressing, and sprinkle with blue cheese, mozzarella, Parmesan, and celery.
4. Continue layering in this order: noodles, buffalo sauce, chicken, ranch dressing, cheeses, celery, until you've used up all your ingredients. Finish with a final layer of buffalo sauce and a generous sprinkle of cheese on top.
5. Cover the baking dish with aluminum foil and bake in the preheated oven for 35 minutes. Remove the foil and bake for an additional 15-20 minutes, or until the cheese is bubbly and golden.
6. Let the lasagna rest for at least 15 minutes before serving.

TOTAL NUTRITIONAL VALUE

Calories: 4,600; Protein: 260g; Carbohydrates: 230g; Fat: 270g; Fiber: 4g; Sugar: 10g

NOTE

Buffalo sauce can be quite spicy. Adjust the amount based on your heat preference. If you want a milder lasagna, consider using half buffalo sauce and half tomato sauce.

RAVIOLI

These delightful little pockets of pasta are a true testament to the creativity and ingenuity of Italian cuisine. Each raviolo (that's the singular form, dear ones) is like a small gift waiting to be unwrapped, revealing the treasures hidden within. Whether they're filled with rich cheeses, succulent meats, or vibrant vegetables, ravioli are a celebration of flavors and textures, all wrapped up in a delicate pasta envelope.

Now, I must confess, making ravioli does require a bit more patience and finesse compared to some other pasta types. But, oh, the rewards are worth every moment spent! When you bite into a perfectly crafted raviolo, with its filling oozing out, complemented by a sauce that ties everything together, you'll understand why this pasta has been cherished for generations.

In the upcoming pages, I'll guide you through the art of making ravioli from scratch. From crafting the perfect dough to mastering the technique of sealing those precious fillings inside, we'll embark on a journey that's as fulfilling as the pasta itself. And, of course, I haven't forgotten about the fillings! We'll explore a range of traditional and innovative fillings that will make your ravioli truly stand out.

Before we dive into the recipes, let's take a moment to understand the process of making ravioli. This will set the foundation for all the delightful variations you'll encounter in the following pages.

<u>Step-by-Step Guide:</u>

SERVING: 16-32 people

INGREDIENTS:

- 300 g "Tipo 00" Flour or all-purpose flour
- 171 g Eggs – about 3 medium eggs

DIRECTIONS:

1. **Mixing the Dough:**
   - On a large, clean work surface or in a large bowl, pour flour into a mound. Create a well in the center that's about 4 inches wide.
   - Gently whisk the eggs using a fork, slowly incorporating the flour from the edges. As the mixture starts coming together, use your hands to fold in the remaining flour until a dough forms.
   - The dough should be firm but not too dry. If it's too sticky, add a sprinkle of flour. If it's too dry and crumbly, you can add a few drops of water.

2. **Kneading:**
   - Press the dough together to form a cohesive ball.
   - Place the dough on a floured surface. Use the heel of your hand to push the dough away from you, then fold it back over itself. Give the dough a quarter turn and repeat for about 8-10 minutes until the dough is smooth and elastic.
   - Once kneaded, shape the dough into a ball and let it rest covered tightly with plastic wrap for at least 30 minutes.

3. **Rolling the Dough:**
   - Divide your dough into manageable pieces, about the size of a lemon and pre-shape it into a rough oval shape.
   - Start at the widest setting on your pasta machine.
   - Feed the dough through the rollers. After the first pass, fold the dough in half or into thirds and pass it through the widest setting again.
   - Gradually reduce the roller setting, passing the dough through each time until you reach the desired thickness.

4. **Fill and cut Ravioli:**
   - Set your pasta maker to setting 6 or 7 if you're using a Mercato Atlas 150, or to setting 4 or 5 if you're using a KitchenAid attachment.
   - Roll the dough through the machine a couple of times to achieve the desired thickness.
   - Once done, gently trim the rounded edges. Cut the dough into sheets that are 10-12 inches long. Place them on a baking sheet and cover with parchment paper. Continue this process with the remaining three pieces of dough.
   - Place filling on a dough sheet: beginners can add four teaspoons spaced two fingers apart. More skilled individuals can create two rows, making eight ravioli per sheet.
   - Using a slightly damp pastry brush, wet the dough around each mound of filling. Place a second sheet of dough over the first, aligning it like a sandwich. Press the dough around each ravioli portion with dry, floured fingers to seal it, taking care not to trap air inside.

- Cut the ravioli into your preferred shape using your chosen tool. Use your fingertips to ensure each pocket of dough is securely sealed along the edges.
- Transfer the finished ravioli to a baking sheet lined with parchment paper and sprinkled with semolina flour. Cover with a towel or another inverted baking sheet. Repeat these steps to assemble and cut the remaining ravioli.

The Filling

While there are countless variations and regional specialties, we've chosen to focus on three of the most classic and beloved fillings. These fillings have graced Italian tables for generations and have found their way into the hearts of many, both in Italy and abroad.

Below, we'll delve into detailed recipes and step-by-step Directions. for crafting these three iconic fillings: Ricotta and Spinach, Butternut Squash, and Beef and Pork. Each filling brings its unique flavor profile and texture, ensuring that there's something for everyone, whether you're a fan of creamy and delicate or hearty and robust.

Ricotta and Spinach Filling

YIELD: Enough for approximately 16 ravioli

INGREDIENTS:
- 1 cup (250g) fresh ricotta cheese
- 1/2 cup (120g) fresh spinach
- 1/4 cup (25g) grated Parmesan cheese
- A pinch of nutmeg
- Salt and pepper, to taste

DIRECTIONS:
1. In a large pan, drizzle some olive oil and heat over medium. Add the spinach, stirring occasionally to ensure even wilting. If the pan is too full, wait for some to wilt before adding more.
2. Once all the spinach is wilted, let it simmer for an additional minute, then turn off the heat.
3. Transfer the spinach to a colander to drain. Once cooled, squeeze out any excess liquid.
4. Roughly chop the drained spinach and set aside.
5. In a mixing bowl, combine the ricotta cheese and finely chopped spinach. Mix until well combined.
6. Add in the grated Parmesan cheese and mix again until smooth.
7. Season with a pinch of nutmeg, salt, and pepper. Adjust the seasoning according to your taste.
8. Once mixed, give it a taste test and adjust the seasoning if necessary.
9. Your filling is now ready to be used in your ravioli. Store any unused portion in an airtight container in the refrigerator for up to 2 days.

Butternut Squash Filling

YIELD: Enough for approximately 16 ravioli

INGREDIENTS:

- 1 small butternut squash (about 1 lb or 450g)
- 1/4 cup (25g) grated Parmesan cheese
- 2 tablespoons breadcrumbs
- 1 tablespoon fresh sage, finely chopped
- Salt and pepper, to taste
- Olive oil, for roasting

DIRECTIONS:

1. Preheat your oven to 400°F (200°C). Cut the butternut squash in half lengthwise and scoop out the seeds. Drizzle the cut sides with olive oil and season with salt and pepper.
2. Place the squash halves cut-side down on a baking sheet lined with parchment paper. Roast in the oven for about 30-40 minutes, or until the squash is tender and can be easily pierced with a fork.
3. Remove from the oven and let it cool slightly. Once cool enough to handle, scoop out the flesh of the squash and discard the skin.
4. In a mixing bowl, combine the roasted butternut squash, grated Parmesan cheese, breadcrumbs, and chopped sage. Mash everything together until you achieve a smooth consistency. Season with salt and pepper to taste.
5. Your butternut squash filling is now ready to be used in your ravioli!

Beef and Pork Filling

Yield: Enough for approximately 16 ravioli

INGREDIENTS:

- 1/4 lb (113g) ground beef
- 1/4 lb (113g) ground pork
- 1 small onion, finely chopped (about 1/2 cup or 75g)
- 2 cloves garlic, minced
- 2 tablespoons breadcrumbs
- 1 egg, lightly beaten
- 1/4 cup (25g) grated Parmesan cheese
- Salt and pepper, to taste
- 1 tablespoon olive oil, for sautéing

DIRECTIONS:

1. In a large skillet, heat the olive oil over medium heat. Add the chopped onion and sauté until translucent, about 2-3 minutes. Add the minced garlic and sauté for another minute.
2. Add the ground beef and pork to the skillet. Cook, breaking apart the meat with a spatula, until browned and cooked through. Season with salt and pepper.
3. Remove from heat and transfer the meat mixture to a mixing bowl. Allow it to cool slightly.
4. To the cooled meat mixture, add the breadcrumbs, beaten egg, and grated Parmesan cheese. Mix until all ingredients are well combined and the mixture holds together.
5. Your beef and pork filling is now ready to be used in your ravioli!

<u>How to cook ravioli:</u>

1. Start by filling a large pot with water and setting it on medium heat. Wait for it to come to a rolling boil.
2. Once the water is boiling, add a tablespoon of salt. This step is crucial as it helps to season the ravioli and enhance their overall flavor.
3. Carefully place the ravioli into the boiling water. It's best to cook them in batches, adding about 8-12 ravioli at a time to prevent them from sticking together.
4. Allow the ravioli to cook for approximately 3-4 minutes. You'll know they're done when they rise to the surface of the water.
5. Using a slotted spoon, remove the ravioli from the water, letting any excess water drip off. You can then transfer them to a plate or directly into your preferred sauce, ensuring they're well-coated and flavorful.

RAVIOLI WITH BROWN BUTTER & SAGE SAUCE

SERVES:16-32   PREP: 30 min   COOK: 15 min

INGREDIENTS

For the Dough:
- 300g "Tipo 00" Flour or all-purpose flour
- 171g Eggs – about 3 medium eggs

For the Filling:
- 1 cup (250g) fresh ricotta cheese
- 1/2 cup (120g) fresh spinach
- 1/4 cup (25g) grated Parmesan cheese
- A pinch of nutmeg
- Salt and pepper, to taste

For the Sauce:
- 1/2 cup (115g) unsalted butter
- 10-12 fresh sage leaves
- Salt and pepper, to taste
- 1/4 cup (25g) grated Parmesan cheese
- Toasted pine nuts
- Additional grated Parmesan

TOTAL NUTRITIONAL VALUE

Calories: 5200; Protein: 200g; Carbohydrates: 360g; Fat: 336g; Fiber: 16g; Sugar: 8g

DIRECTIONS

1. Prepare the dough using the listed ingredients and create a ravioli sheet following the step-by-step Directions.
2. Prepare the filling and season the ravioli following the Directions. given earlier.
3. In a skillet over medium heat, melt the butter. Once it starts to foam, add the sage leaves. Continue to cook until the butter turns a light brown color and has a nutty aroma. Remove from heat and season with salt, pepper, and grated Parmesan.
4. Cook the ravioli in batches (8-12 at a time) in boiling salted water until they float to the top. Using a slotted spoon, transfer the ravioli to the skillet with the brown butter and sage sauce. Gently toss to coat.
5. Serve the ravioli on plates, garnished with toasted pine nuts and additional grated Parmesan.

NOTE

For an added crunch, toast the pine nuts until golden before garnishing. This enhances their nutty flavor and complements the richness of the brown butter.

RAVIOLI WITH TOMATO BASIL SAUCE

 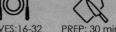

SERVES:16-32   PREP: 30 min   COOK: 20 min

INGREDIENTS

For the Dough:
- 300g "Tipo 00" Flour or all-purpose flour
- 171g Eggs – about 3 medium eggs

For the Filling:
- 1 cup (250g) fresh ricotta cheese
- 1/2 cup (120g) fresh spinach
- 1/4 cup (25g) grated Parmesan cheese
- A pinch of nutmeg
- Salt and pepper, to taste

For the Sauce:
- 1 can (28 oz) crushed tomatoes
- 1/2 cup fresh basil leaves, chopped
- 3 cloves garlic, minced
- 2 tbsp olive oil
- Salt and pepper, to taste
- Fresh basil leaves
- Grated Parmesan cheese

TOTAL NUTRITIONAL VALUE

Calories: 3200; Protein: 160g; Carbohydrates: 420g; Fat: 100g; Fiber: 28g; Sugar: 40g

DIRECTIONS

1. Prepare the dough using the listed ingredients and create a ravioli sheet following the step-by-step Directions.
2. Prepare the filling and season the ravioli following the Directions. given earlier.
3. In a skillet over medium heat, warm the olive oil. Add the minced garlic and sauté until fragrant. Add the crushed tomatoes and bring to a simmer. Cook for 10-15 minutes, then stir in the chopped basil. Season with salt and pepper.
4. Cook the ravioli in batches (8-12 at a time) in boiling salted water until they float to the top. Using a slotted spoon, transfer the ravioli to the skillet with the tomato basil sauce. Gently toss to coat.
5. Serve the ravioli on plates, garnished with fresh basil leaves and a sprinkle of grated Parmesan.

RAVIOLI WITH CREAMY GARLIC SPINACH SAUCE

SERVES:16-32   PREP: 30 min   COOK: 20 min

INGREDIENTS

For the Dough:
- 300g "Tipo 00" Flour or all-purpose flour
- 171g Eggs – about 3 medium eggs

For the Filling:
- 1 cup (250g) fresh ricotta cheese
- 1/2 cup (120g) fresh spinach
- 1/4 cup (25g) grated Parmesan cheese
- A pinch of nutmeg
- Salt and pepper, to taste

For the Sauce:
- 3 cloves garlic, minced
- 1 cup (240g) fresh spinach, chopped
- 1 cup (240ml) heavy cream
- 1/2 cup (50g) grated Parmesan cheese
- Salt and pepper, to taste
- 2 tbsp olive oil
- Red pepper flakes
- Additional grated Parmesan

TOTAL NUTRITIONAL VALUE

Calories: 3800; Protein: 180g; Carbohydrates: 380g; Fat: 200g; Fiber: 12g; Sugar: 12g

DIRECTIONS

1. Prepare the dough using the listed ingredients and create a ravioli sheet following the step-by-step Directions.
2. Prepare the filling and season the ravioli following the Directions. given earlier.
3. In a skillet over medium heat, warm the olive oil. Add the minced garlic and sauté until fragrant. Add the chopped spinach and cook until wilted. Pour in the heavy cream and bring to a simmer. Stir in the grated Parmesan and season with salt and pepper.
4. Cook the ravioli in batches (8-12 at a time) in boiling salted water until they float to the top. Using a slotted spoon, transfer the ravioli to the skillet with the creamy garlic and spinach sauce. Gently toss to coat.
5. Serve the ravioli on plates, garnished with red pepper flakes and additional grated Parmesan.

RAVIOLI WITH MAPLE BROWN BUTTER SAUCE

SERVES:16-32   PREP: 40 min   COOK: 20 min

INGREDIENTS

For the Dough:
- 300g "Tipo 00" Flour or all-purpose flour
- 171g Eggs – about 3 medium eggs

For the Filling:
- 1 small butternut squash (about 1 lb or 450g)
- 1/4 cup (25g) grated Parmesan cheese
- 2 tablespoons breadcrumbs
- 1 tablespoon fresh sage, finely chopped
- Salt and pepper, to taste
- Olive oil, for roasting

For the Sauce:
- 1/2 cup (115g) unsalted butter
- 3 tablespoons maple syrup
- 6 fresh sage leaves
- Salt and pepper, to taste
- 1/4 cup (30g) toasted pecans
- 1/4 cup (40g) crumbled feta cheese

TOTAL NUTRITIONAL VALUE

Calories: 2800; Protein: 80g; Carbohydrates: 320g; Fat: 150g; Fiber: 20g; Sugar: 60g

DIRECTIONS

1. Prepare the dough using the listed ingredients and create a ravioli sheet following the step-by-step Directions.
2. Prepare the filling and season the ravioli following the Directions. given earlier.
3. In a skillet over medium heat, melt the butter. Once it starts to foam, add the sage leaves. Cook until the butter turns a light brown color and has a nutty aroma. Remove from heat and stir in the maple syrup. Season with salt and pepper.
4. Cook the ravioli in batches (8-12 at a time) until they float to the top.
5. Gently toss the cooked ravioli in the maple brown butter sauce.
6. Serve garnished with toasted pecans and crumbled feta cheese.

RAVIOLI WITH GORGONZOLA CREAM SAUCE

SERVES:16-32   PREP: 40 min   COOK: 20 min

INGREDIENTS

For the Dough:
- 300g "Tipo 00" Flour or all-purpose flour
- 171g Eggs – about 3 medium eggs

For the Filling:
- 1 small butternut squash (about 1 lb or 450g)
- 1/4 cup (25g) grated Parmesan cheese
- 2 tablespoons breadcrumbs
- 1 tablespoon fresh sage, finely chopped
- Salt and pepper, to taste
- Olive oil, for roasting

For the Sauce:
- 1 cup (240ml) heavy cream
- 1/2 cup (60g) crumbled Gorgonzola cheese
- Salt and pepper, to taste
- Chopped fresh parsley
- 1/4 cup (30g) toasted walnuts

DIRECTIONS

1. Prepare the dough using the listed ingredients and create a ravioli sheet following the step-by-step Directions.
2. Prepare the filling and season the ravioli following the Directions. given earlier.
3. In a skillet over medium heat, warm the heavy cream. Once it begins to simmer, reduce the heat and stir in the crumbled Gorgonzola cheese until melted and smooth. Season with salt and pepper.
4. Cook the ravioli in batches (8-12 at a time) until they float to the top.
5. Gently toss the cooked ravioli in the Gorgonzola cream sauce.
6. Serve garnished with chopped fresh parsley and toasted walnuts.

TOTAL NUTRITIONAL VALUE

Calories: 2900; Protein: 90g; Carbohydrates: 310g; Fat: 170g; Fiber: 18g; Sugar: 8g

RAVIOLI WITH ROASTED GARLIC & ROSEMARY OLIVE OIL

SERVES:16-32   PREP: 45 min   COOK: 20 min

INGREDIENTS

For the Dough:
- 300g "Tipo 00" Flour or all-purpose flour
- 171g Eggs – about 3 medium eggs

For the Filling:
- 1 small butternut squash (about 1 lb or 450g)
- 1/4 cup (25g) grated Parmesan cheese
- 2 tablespoons breadcrumbs
- 1 tablespoon fresh sage, finely chopped
- Salt and pepper, to taste
- Olive oil, for roasting

For the Sauce:
- 1/2 cup (120ml) olive oil
- 8 cloves roasted garlic, mashed
- 2 tablespoons fresh rosemary, finely chopped
- Salt and pepper, to taste
- Grated Parmesan cheese

DIRECTIONS

1. Prepare the dough using the listed ingredients and create a ravioli sheet following the step-by-step Directions.
2. Prepare the filling and season the ravioli following the Directions. given earlier.
3. In a skillet over low heat, warm the olive oil. Add the mashed roasted garlic and rosemary, stirring until fragrant. Season with salt and pepper.
4. Cook the ravioli in batches (8-12 at a time) until they float to the top.
5. Gently toss the cooked ravioli in the roasted garlic and rosemary olive oil.
6. Serve garnished with grated Parmesan cheese.

TOTAL NUTRITIONAL VALUE

Calories: 2700; Protein: 75g; Carbohydrates: 300g; Fat: 150g; Fiber: 18g; Sugar: 6g

RAVIOLI IN BROTH

SERVES:16-32   PREP: 45 min   COOK: 25 min

INGREDIENTS

For the Dough:
- 300g "Tipo 00" Flour or all-purpose flour
- 171g Eggs – about 3 medium eggs

For the Filling:
- 1/4 lb (113g) ground beef
- 1/4 lb (113g) ground pork
- 1 small onion, finely chopped (about 1/2 cup or 75g)
- 2 cloves garlic, minced
- 2 tablespoons breadcrumbs
- 1 egg, lightly beaten
- 1/4 cup (25g) grated Parmesan cheese
- Salt and pepper, to taste
- 1 tablespoon olive oil, for sautéing
- Grated Parmesan cheese
- Freshly ground black pepper

For the Broth:
- 8 cups (1.9 liters) beef or chicken broth
- 2 tablespoons fresh parsley, finely chopped
- Salt and pepper, to taste

TOTAL NUTRITIONAL VALUE

Calories: 2300; Protein: 130g; Carbohydrates: 240g; Fat: 80g; Fiber: 10g; Sugar: 8g

DIRECTIONS

1. Prepare the dough using the listed ingredients and create a ravioli sheet following the step-by-step Directions.
2. Prepare the filling and season the ravioli following the Directions. given earlier.
3. In a large pot, bring the beef or chicken broth to a simmer. Add the fresh parsley, salt, and pepper, adjusting to taste.
4. Add the ravioli directly to the simmering broth, cooking them in batches (8-12 at a time) until they float to the top.
5. Gently transfer the cooked ravioli to serving bowls and ladle the hot broth over them.
6. Serve garnished with grated Parmesan cheese and freshly ground black pepper.

RAVIOLI WITH CLASSIC MARINARA SAUCE

SERVES:16-32   PREP: 45 min   COOK: 30 min

INGREDIENTS

For the Dough:
- 300g "Tipo 00" Flour or all-purpose flour
- 171g Eggs – about 3 medium eggs

For the Filling:
- 1/4 lb (113g) ground beef
- 1/4 lb (113g) ground pork
- 1 small onion, finely chopped (about 1/2 cup or 75g)
- 2 cloves garlic, minced
- 2 tablespoons breadcrumbs
- 1 egg, lightly beaten
- 1/4 cup (25g) grated Parmesan cheese
- Salt and pepper, to taste
- 1 tablespoon olive oil, for sautéing

For the Sauce:
- 1 can (28 oz) crushed tomatoes
- 2 cloves garlic, minced
- 2 tablespoons olive oil
- 1/4 cup fresh basil, chopped
- Salt and pepper, to taste
- Fresh basil leaves
- Grated Parmesan cheese

TOTAL NUTRITIONAL VALUE

Calories: 1450; Protein: 60g; Carbohydrates: 170g; Fat: 60g; Fiber: 10g; Sugar: 12g

DIRECTIONS

1. Prepare the dough using the listed ingredients and create a ravioli sheet following the step-by-step Directions.
2. Prepare the filling and season the ravioli following the Directions. given earlier.
3. In a large skillet, heat the olive oil over medium heat. Add the minced garlic and sauté until fragrant, about 1 minute. Add the crushed tomatoes, salt, and pepper. Let the sauce simmer for 20 minutes, stirring occasionally. Add the chopped basil in the last 5 minutes of cooking.
4. In a large pot of boiling salted water, cook the ravioli in batches (8-12 at a time) until they float to the top.
5. Serve the ravioli with the marinara sauce, garnished with fresh basil leaves and a sprinkle of grated Parmesan cheese.

RAVIOLI WITH CREAMY MUSHROOM SAUCE

SERVES: 16-32 PREP: 45 min COOK: 35 min

INGREDIENTS

For the Dough:
- 300g "Tipo 00" Flour or all-purpose flour
- 171g Eggs – about 3 medium eggs

For the Filling:
- 1/4 lb (113g) ground beef
- 1/4 lb (113g) ground pork
- 1 small onion, finely chopped (about 1/2 cup or 75g)
- 2 cloves garlic, minced
- 2 tablespoons breadcrumbs
- 1 egg, lightly beaten
- 1/4 cup (25g) grated Parmesan cheese
- Salt and pepper, to taste
- 1 tablespoon olive oil, for sautéing

For the Sauce:
- 1 cup (about 150g) mushrooms, sliced
- 2 cloves garlic, minced
- 1/2 cup heavy cream
- 1/4 cup white wine
- Salt and pepper, to taste
- 2 tablespoons olive oil
- Chopped fresh parsley
- Grated Parmesan cheese

DIRECTIONS

1. Prepare the dough using the listed ingredients and create a ravioli sheet following the step-by-step Directions.
2. Prepare the filling and season the ravioli following the Directions. given earlier.
3. In a large skillet, heat the olive oil over medium heat. Add the sliced mushrooms and sauté until they release their moisture and begin to brown. Add the minced garlic and sauté for another minute.
4. Pour in the white wine and let it reduce by half. Add the heavy cream, salt, and pepper, and let the sauce simmer until it thickens slightly.
5. In a large pot of boiling salted water, cook the ravioli in batches (8-12 at a time) until they float to the top.
6. Serve the ravioli with the creamy mushroom sauce, garnished with chopped parsley and a sprinkle of grated Parmesan cheese.

TOTAL NUTRITIONAL VALUE

Calories: 1650; Protein: 65g; Carbohydrates: 180g; Fat: 80g; Fiber: 12g; Sugar: 8g

RAVIOLI WITH SPICY ARRABBIATA SAUCE

SERVES: 16-32 PREP: 45 min COOK: 30 min

INGREDIENTS

For the Dough:
- 300g "Tipo 00" Flour or all-purpose flour
- 171g Eggs – about 3 medium eggs

For the Filling:
- 1/4 lb (113g) ground beef
- 1/4 lb (113g) ground pork
- 1 small onion, finely chopped (about 1/2 cup or 75g)
- 2 cloves garlic, minced
- 2 tablespoons breadcrumbs
- 1 egg, lightly beaten
- 1/4 cup (25g) grated Parmesan cheese
- Salt and pepper, to taste
- 1 tablespoon olive oil, for sautéing

For the Sauce:
- 1 can (28 oz) crushed tomatoes
- 3 cloves garlic, minced
- 1-2 teaspoons red pepper flakes (adjust to desired spiciness)
- 2 tablespoons olive oil
- Salt and pepper, to taste
- Fresh basil, chopped (for flavor and garnish)
- Fresh parsley, chopped
- Grated Parmesan cheese

DIRECTIONS

1. Prepare the dough using the listed ingredients and create a ravioli sheet following the step-by-step Directions.
2. Prepare the filling and season the ravioli following the Directions. given earlier.
3. In a large skillet, heat the olive oil over medium heat. Add the minced garlic and red pepper flakes, sautéing briefly until fragrant but not browned.
4. Add the crushed tomatoes, salt, and pepper. Let the sauce simmer for about 20 minutes, allowing the flavors to meld. Stir in the chopped basil a few minutes before the sauce is done.
5. In a large pot of boiling salted water, cook the ravioli in batches (8-12 at a time) until they float to the top.
6. Serve the ravioli with the spicy arrabbiata sauce, garnished with fresh parsley and a sprinkle of grated Parmesan cheese.

TOTAL NUTRITIONAL VALUE

Calories: 1500; Protein: 65g; Carbohydrates: 175g; Fat: 65g; Fiber: 11g; Sugar: 12g

CAPELLINI

Hailing from the diverse culinary landscapes of Italy, capellini, often referred to as "angel hair," is the epitome of delicacy and finesse in the world of pasta. Its name, translating to "little hairs," perfectly encapsulates its thin and elegant strands.

Capellini's slender nature allows it to cook swiftly, making it an ideal choice for those moments when time is of the essence, yet flavor cannot be compromised. Its fine texture pairs beautifully with light, fragrant sauces, be it a simple toss of fresh tomatoes and basil or a gentle drizzle of garlic-infused olive oil.

As we delve into the recipes that lie ahead, let capellini's ethereal nature guide your culinary senses. Each bite, light yet flavorful, is a testament to the artistry and precision of Italian pasta-making, reminding us that sometimes, the simplest ingredients, when crafted with care, can create the most profound gastronomic experiences.

Step-by-Step Guide:

SERVING: 4-6 people

INGREDIENTS:

- 400 g "Tipo 00" Flour or all-purpose flour
- 228 g Eggs – about four medium eggs

DIRECTIONS:

1. **Mixing the Dough:**
   - On a large, clean work surface or in a large bowl, pour flour into a mound. Create a well in the center that's about 4 inches wide.
   - Gently whisk the eggs using a fork, slowly incorporating the flour from the edges. As the mixture starts coming together, use your hands to fold in the remaining flour until a dough forms.
   - The dough should be firm but not too dry. If it's too sticky, add a sprinkle of flour. If it's too dry and crumbly, you can add a few drops of water.

2. **Kneading:**
   - Press the dough together to form a cohesive ball.
   - Place the dough on a floured surface. Use the heel of your hand to push the dough away from you, then fold it back over itself. Give the dough a quarter turn and repeat for about 8-10 minutes until the dough is smooth and elastic.
   - Once kneaded, shape the dough into a ball and let it rest covered tightly with plastic wrap for at least 30 minutes.

3. **Rolling the Dough:**
   - Divide your dough into manageable pieces, about the size of a lemon and pre-shape it into a rough oval shape.
   - Start at the widest setting on your pasta machine.
   - Feed the dough through the rollers. After the first pass, fold the dough in half or into thirds and pass it through the widest setting again.
   - Gradually reduce the roller setting, passing the dough through each time until you reach the desired thickness.

4. **Fill and cut Capellini:**
   - Set your pasta maker to setting 8 or 9 if you're using a Mercato Atlas, or to setting 7 or 8 if you're using a KitchenAid attachment.
   - Roll the dough through the machine a couple of times to achieve the desired thickness.
   - Place the rolled dough on a floured surface and leave to dry for 10-15 minutes.
   - Attach the capellini cutter to your pasta maker.
   - Feed the pasta sheets through the capellini attachment.
   - As the capellini emerges, collect it in a bowl with a bit of flour, gently tossing to prevent sticking.
   - Lay the finished capellini on a dry tea towel.

SPINACH CAPELLINI WITH FRESH TOMATO AND BASIL SAUCE

SERVES: 4-6 PREP: 20 min COOK: 25 min

INGREDIENTS

For the Dough:
- 280g "Tipo 00" Flour or all-purpose flour
- 5 yolks from 5 large eggs (90g)
- 1 whole large egg (57g)
- 56g spinach purée

For the Seasoning:
- 4 ripe tomatoes, diced
- 2 garlic cloves, minced
- 1/4 cup (60 ml) extra virgin olive oil
- 1/4 cup (10g) fresh basil leaves, chopped
- Salt and freshly ground black pepper, to taste
- Grated Parmesan cheese, for serving

DIRECTIONS

1. Prepare the dough using the listed ingredients and shape into capellini following the step-by-step Directions.
2. In a large skillet, heat olive oil over medium heat. Add the minced garlic and sauté until fragrant.
3. Add the diced tomatoes to the skillet and cook until they soften and release their juices.
4. Stir in the chopped basil and season with salt and pepper.
5. Meanwhile, cook the spinach capellini in a large pot of boiling salted water until al dente. Before draining the pasta, reserve about 1/2 cup (120 ml) of the cooking water.
6. Drain the capellini and add to the skillet with the fresh tomato and basil sauce. If the sauce is too thick or if you desire a glossier sauce, gradually add the reserved cooking water until you reach the desired consistency.
7. Toss to combine and serve with freshly grated Parmesan cheese.

TOTAL NUTRITIONAL VALUE

Calories: 2,100; Protein: 70g; Carbohydrates: 260g;
Fat: 80g; Fiber: 8g; Sugar: 10g

CAPELLINI WITH GARLIC SHRIMP AND WHITE WINE SAUCE

SERVES: 4-6 PREP: 20 min COOK: 30 min

INGREDIENTS

For the Dough:
- 400g "Tipo 00" Flour or all-purpose flour
- 228g Eggs – about four medium eggs

For the Seasoning:
- 1 lb (450g) large shrimp, peeled and deveined
- 3 garlic cloves, minced
- 1/4 cup (60 ml) white wine
- 1/4 cup (60 ml) chicken or vegetable broth
- 1/4 cup (60 g) fresh parsley, chopped
- 1/4 cup (60 ml) extra virgin olive oil
- Salt and freshly ground black pepper, to taste
- Red pepper flakes, optional, for a bit of heat

DIRECTIONS

1. Prepare the dough using the listed ingredients and shape into capellini following the step-by-step Directions.
2. In a large skillet, heat olive oil over medium heat. Add the minced garlic and sauté until fragrant.
3. Add the shrimp to the skillet and cook until they turn pink and are cooked through.
4. Pour in the white wine and broth, allowing it to simmer and reduce by half.
5. Stir in the chopped parsley and season with salt, black pepper, and red pepper flakes if using.
6. Meanwhile, cook the capellini in a large pot of boiling salted water until al dente. Before draining the pasta, reserve about 1/2 cup (120 ml) of the cooking water.
7. Drain the capellini and add to the skillet with the garlic shrimp and white wine sauce. If the sauce is too thick or if you desire a glossier sauce, gradually add the reserved cooking water until you reach the desired consistency.
8. Toss to combine and serve immediately.

TOTAL NUTRITIONAL VALUE

Calories: 2,400; Protein: 90g; Carbohydrates: 280g;
Fat: 90g; Fiber: 2g; Sugar: 3g

CAPELLINI WITH OLIVE TAPENADE AND CHERRY TOMATOES

SERVES: 4-6   PREP: 20 min   COOK: 20 min

INGREDIENTS

For the Dough:
- 400g "Tipo 00" Flour or all-purpose flour
- 228g Eggs – about four medium eggs

For the Seasoning:
- 1 cup (240 ml) olive tapenade (store-bought or homemade)
- 1 cup (150g) cherry tomatoes, halved
- 3 garlic cloves, minced
- 1/4 cup (60 ml) extra virgin olive oil
- Salt and freshly ground black pepper, to taste
- Fresh basil or parsley, chopped, for garnish
- Grated Parmesan cheese, for serving

DIRECTIONS

1. Prepare the dough using the listed ingredients and shape into capellini following the step-by-step Directions.
2. In a large skillet, heat olive oil over medium heat. Add the minced garlic and sauté until fragrant.
3. Stir in the olive tapenade and cherry tomatoes, cooking until the tomatoes are slightly softened.
4. Meanwhile, cook the capellini in a large pot of boiling salted water until al dente. Before draining the pasta, reserve about 1/2 cup (120 ml) of the cooking water.
5. Drain the capellini and add to the skillet with the olive tapenade and cherry tomatoes. If the mixture is too thick or if you desire a glossier sauce, gradually add the reserved cooking water until you reach the desired consistency.
6. Season with salt and pepper. Serve garnished with chopped fresh basil or parsley and freshly grated Parmesan cheese.

TOTAL NUTRITIONAL VALUE

Calories: 2,300; Protein: 70g; Carbohydrates: 270g; Fat: 110g; Fiber: 6g; Sugar: 6g

CAPELLINI CACIO E PEPE (CHEESE AND BLACK PEPPER)

SERVES: 4-6   PREP: 10 min   COOK: 15 min

INGREDIENTS

For the Dough:
- 400g "Tipo 00" Flour or all-purpose flour
- 228g Eggs – about four medium eggs

For the Seasoning:
- 1 cup (100g) Pecorino Romano cheese, freshly grated
- 1 tsp freshly ground black pepper
- 1/4 cup (60 g) unsalted butter
- Salt, to taste

DIRECTIONS

1. Prepare the dough using the listed ingredients and shape into capellini following the step-by-step Directions.
2. In a large skillet, melt the butter over low heat. Add the freshly ground black pepper and stir.
3. Meanwhile, cook the capellini in a large pot of boiling salted water until al dente. Before draining the pasta, reserve about 1/2 cup (120 ml) of the cooking water.
4. Drain the capellini and add to the skillet with the butter and pepper. Add the grated Pecorino Romano cheese and toss, gradually adding the reserved cooking water until you achieve a creamy consistency that coats the pasta.
5. Season with salt if needed. Serve immediately with additional Pecorino Romano cheese on top if desired.

TOTAL NUTRITIONAL VALUE

Calories: 2,200; Protein: 80g; Carbohydrates: 260g; Fat: 90g; Fiber: 2g; Sugar: 2g

TOMATO CAPELLINI WITH BASIL, MOZZARELLA, AND BALSAMIC REDUCTION

SERVES: 4-6   PREP: 25 min   COOK: 30 min

INGREDIENTS

For the Dough:
- 280g "Tipo 00" Flour or all-purpose flour
- 5 yolks from 5 large eggs (90g)
- 1 whole large egg (57g)
- 56g tomato paste

For the Seasoning:
- 1 cup (240 ml) balsamic vinegar
- 1 cup (150g) cherry tomatoes, halved
- 1 cup (150g) fresh mozzarella balls or cubes
- 1/4 cup (10g) fresh basil leaves, torn
- 1/4 cup (60 ml) extra virgin olive oil
- Salt and freshly ground black pepper, to taste

DIRECTIONS

1. Prepare the dough using the listed ingredients and shape into capellini following the step-by-step Directions.
2. In a small saucepan, simmer the balsamic vinegar over low heat until it reduces by half and thickens, about 15 minutes. Set aside to cool.
3. In a large skillet, heat olive oil over medium heat. Add the cherry tomatoes and sauté until they are slightly softened.
4. Meanwhile, cook the orange tomato capellini in a large pot of boiling salted water until al dente. Before draining the pasta, reserve about 1/2 cup (120 ml) of the cooking water.
5. Drain the capellini and add to the skillet with the cherry tomatoes. Toss to combine. If you desire a glossier sauce, gradually add the reserved cooking water until you reach the desired consistency.
6. Season with salt and pepper. Serve topped with fresh mozzarella, torn basil leaves, and a drizzle of the balsamic reduction.

TOTAL NUTRITIONAL VALUE

Calories: 2,400; Protein: 85g; Carbohydrates: 280g;
Fat: 100g; Fiber: 5g; Sugar: 12g

CAPELLINI WITH ASPARAGUS, LEMON ZEST, AND PINE NUTS

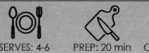

SERVES: 4-6   PREP: 20 min   COOK: 25 min

INGREDIENTS

For the Dough:
- 400g "Tipo 00" Flour or all-purpose flour
- 228g Eggs – about four medium eggs

For the Seasoning:
- 1 bunch of asparagus, trimmed and cut into 1-inch pieces
- Zest of 1 lemon
- 1/4 cup (60 ml) extra virgin olive oil
- 1/4 cup (35g) pine nuts, toasted
- Salt and freshly ground black pepper, to taste
- Grated Parmesan cheese, for serving

DIRECTIONS

1. Prepare the dough using the listed ingredients and shape into capellini following the step-by-step Directions.
2. In a large skillet, heat olive oil over medium heat. Add the asparagus pieces and sauté until they are tender but still have a slight crunch.
3. Stir in the lemon zest and toasted pine nuts.
4. Meanwhile, cook the capellini in a large pot of boiling salted water until al dente. Before draining the pasta, reserve about 1/2 cup (120 ml) of the cooking water.
5. Drain the capellini and add to the skillet with the asparagus, lemon zest, and pine nuts. If the mixture is too dry or if you desire a glossier sauce, gradually add the reserved cooking water until you reach the desired consistency.
6. Season with salt and pepper. Serve with freshly grated Parmesan cheese on top.

TOTAL NUTRITIONAL VALUE

Calories: 2,300; Protein: 75g; Carbohydrates: 270g;
Fat: 110g; Fiber: 6g; Sugar: 4g

CAPELLINI WITH PROSCIUTTO, PEAS, AND PARMESAN

SERVES: 4-6   PREP: 20 min   COOK: 25 min

INGREDIENTS

For the Dough:
- 400g "Tipo 00" Flour or all-purpose flour
- 228g Eggs – about four medium eggs

For the Seasoning:
- 1/2 cup (120g) prosciutto, thinly sliced and torn into pieces
- 1 cup (150g) fresh or frozen peas
- 1/4 cup (60 ml) extra virgin olive oil
- 1/2 cup (50g) Parmesan cheese, freshly grated
- Salt and freshly ground black pepper, to taste

DIRECTIONS

1. Prepare the dough using the listed ingredients and shape into capellini following the step-by-step Directions.
2. In a large skillet, heat olive oil over medium heat. Add the prosciutto pieces and sauté until they are slightly crispy.
3. Add the peas to the skillet and cook until they are tender. If using frozen peas, cook until they are heated through.
4. Meanwhile, cook the capellini in a large pot of boiling salted water until al dente. Before draining the pasta, reserve about 1/2 cup (120 ml) of the cooking water.
5. Drain the capellini and add to the skillet with the prosciutto and peas. Toss to combine. If the mixture is too dry or if you desire a glossier sauce, gradually add the reserved cooking water until you reach the desired consistency.
6. Season with salt and pepper. Serve topped with freshly grated Parmesan cheese.

TOTAL NUTRITIONAL VALUE

Calories: 2,350; Protein: 80g; Carbohydrates: 270g;
Fat: 105g; Fiber: 5g; Sugar: 5g

CAPELLINI WITH ANCHOVIES, CAPERS, AND FRESH PARSLEY

SERVES: 4-6   PREP: 15 min   COOK: 20 min

INGREDIENTS

For the Dough:
- 400g "Tipo 00" Flour or all-purpose flour
- 228g Eggs – about four medium eggs

For the Seasoning:
- 1/4 cup (60 ml) extra virgin olive oil
- 6 anchovy fillets, minced
- 2 tbsp capers, drained and rinsed
- 1/4 cup (10g) fresh parsley, chopped
- 2 garlic cloves, minced
- Red pepper flakes, to taste (optional)
- Salt and freshly ground black pepper, to taste

DIRECTIONS

1. Prepare the dough using the listed ingredients and shape into capellini following the step-by-step Directions.
2. In a large skillet, heat olive oil over medium heat. Add the minced garlic and anchovy fillets. Sauté until the garlic is golden and the anchovies have melted into the oil.
3. Stir in the capers and red pepper flakes if using.
4. Meanwhile, cook the capellini in a large pot of boiling salted water until al dente. Before draining the pasta, reserve about 1/2 cup (120 ml) of the cooking water.
5. Drain the capellini and add to the skillet with the anchovy and caper mixture. Toss to combine. If the mixture is too dry or if you desire a glossier sauce, gradually add the reserved cooking water until you reach the desired consistency.
6. Season with salt and pepper. Serve garnished with chopped fresh parsley.

TOTAL NUTRITIONAL VALUE

Calories: 2,200; Protein: 70g; Carbohydrates: 260g;
Fat: 100g; Fiber: 2g; Sugar: 2g

CAPELLINI WITH ROASTED EGGPLANT AND RICOTTA SALATA

SERVES: 4-6   PREP: 25 min   COOK: 35 min

INGREDIENTS

For the Dough:
- 400g "Tipo 00" Flour or all-purpose flour
- 228g Eggs – about four medium eggs

For the Seasoning:
- 1 medium eggplant, diced into 1/2-inch cubes
- 1/4 cup (60 ml) extra virgin olive oil, plus more for drizzling
- 1/2 cup (60g) ricotta salata, crumbled
- 2 garlic cloves, minced
- Salt and freshly ground black pepper, to taste
- Fresh basil leaves, for garnish

DIRECTIONS

1. Preheat the oven to 425°F (220°C). Toss the diced eggplant with olive oil, salt, and pepper. Spread on a baking sheet and roast for 20-25 minutes, or until golden and tender.
2. Prepare the dough using the listed ingredients and shape into capellini following the step-by-step Directions.
3. In a large skillet, heat olive oil over medium heat. Add the minced garlic and sauté until fragrant.
4. Add the roasted eggplant to the skillet and toss to combine.
5. Meanwhile, cook the capellini in a large pot of boiling salted water until al dente. Before draining the pasta, reserve about 1/2 cup (120 ml) of the cooking water.
6. Drain the capellini and add to the skillet with the roasted eggplant. Toss to combine. If the mixture is too dry or if you desire a glossier sauce, gradually add the reserved cooking water until you reach the desired consistency.
7. Season with additional salt and pepper if needed. Serve topped with crumbled ricotta salata and fresh basil leaves.

TOTAL NUTRITIONAL VALUE

Calories: 2,250; Protein: 75g; Carbohydrates: 270g;
Fat: 105g; Fiber: 7g; Sugar: 7g

CAPELLINI WITH TUNA, LEMON, AND ARUGULA

SERVES: 4-6   PREP: 20 min   COOK: 25 min

INGREDIENTS

For the Dough:
- 400g "Tipo 00" Flour or all-purpose flour
- 228g Eggs – about four medium eggs

For the Seasoning:
- 1 can (5 oz/140g) tuna in olive oil, drained
- Zest and juice of 1 lemon
- 2 cups (60g) fresh arugula
- 1/4 cup (60 ml) extra virgin olive oil
- 2 garlic cloves, minced
- Salt and freshly ground black pepper, to taste
- Grated Parmesan cheese, for serving

DIRECTIONS

1. Prepare the dough using the listed ingredients and shape into capellini following the step-by-step Directions.
2. In a large skillet, heat olive oil over medium heat. Add the minced garlic and sauté until fragrant.
3. Stir in the tuna, breaking it up with a fork. Add the lemon zest and juice, and toss to combine.
4. Meanwhile, cook the capellini in a large pot of boiling salted water until al dente. Before draining the pasta, reserve about 1/2 cup (120 ml) of the cooking water.
5. Drain the capellini and add to the skillet with the tuna mixture. Toss to combine. If the mixture is too dry or if you desire a glossier sauce, gradually add the reserved cooking water until you reach the desired consistency.
6. Stir in the fresh arugula until it's just wilted. Season with salt and pepper. Serve with freshly grated Parmesan cheese on top.

TOTAL NUTRITIONAL VALUE

Calories: 2,200; Protein: 85g; Carbohydrates: 260g;
Fat: 100g; Fiber: 3g; Sugar: 2g

VEGAN PASTA

Ah, the wonders of pasta! It's a dish that has transcended borders, bringing joy to tables worldwide. But what if I told you that the joy of pasta isn't limited to traditional recipes? Welcome to the world of vegan pasta. A realm where the essence of Italian tradition meets the principles of veganism, creating a symphony of flavors that's both delightful and compassionate.

For those who've chosen the vegan path, whether for ethical, health, or any other reasons, I salute you. And for those who haven't, I invite you to try this alternative. Vegan pasta is not just about omitting eggs; it's about exploring a different texture, a unique taste, and most importantly, a new way of expressing love through food.

In the following pages, you'll come to realize that every type of pasta we've explored so far, from the long shape pasta to lasagne and ravioli, can be crafted with this vegan dough. The versatility of vegan pasta is truly remarkable, and the flavors are as rich and authentic as any traditional pasta dish.

Before we delve into the recipes, let's revisit the process of crafting our vegan pasta. Trust me, it's simpler than you think, and the results are absolutely worth it. So, without further ado, let's get started!

Step-by-Step Guide:

SERVING: 4-6 people

INGREDIENTS:

- 150 g "Tipo 00" Flour or all-purpose flour
- 150 g semolina flour or sub more regular flour
- ½ tsp salt
- 150 ml water (room temperature)
- 2 tsp olive oil

DIRECTIONS:

1. **Mixing the Dough:**
   - On a large, clean work surface or in a large bowl, pour flour into a mound. Create a well in the center that's about 4 inches wide.
   - Gently whisk the eggs using a fork, slowly incorporating the flour from the edges. As the mixture starts coming together, use your hands to fold in the remaining flour until a dough forms.
   - The dough should be firm but not too dry. If it's too sticky, add a sprinkle of flour. If it's too dry and crumbly, you can add a few drops of water.

2. **Kneading:**
   - Press the dough together to form a cohesive ball.
   - Place the dough on a floured surface. Use the heel of your hand to push the dough away from you, then fold it back over itself. Give the dough a quarter turn and repeat for about 8-10 minutes until the dough is smooth and elastic.
   - Once kneaded, shape the dough into a ball and let it rest covered tightly with plastic wrap for at least 30 minutes.

3. **Rolling the Dough:**
   - Divide your dough into manageable pieces, about the size of a lemon and pre-shape it into a rough oval shape.
   - Start at the widest setting on your pasta machine.
   - Feed the dough through the rollers. After the first pass, fold the dough in half or into thirds and pass it through the widest setting again.
   - Gradually reduce the roller setting, passing the dough through each time until you reach the desired thickness.

4. **Choose the Shape**
   - Roll out the sheet to the right thickness with respect to the type of pasta you have chosen.

VEGAN SPAGHETTI WITH BROCCOLI RABE AND CHILI FLAKES

SERVES: 4-6 PREP: 20 min COOK: 15 min

INGREDIENTS

For the Dough:
- 150 g "Tipo 00" Flour or all-purpose flour
- 150 g semolina flour (or substitute with more regular flour)
- ½ tsp salt
- 150 ml water (room temperature)
- 2 tsp olive oil

For the Seasoning:
- 1 bunch Broccoli Rabe, trimmed and chopped
- 3 tbsp Olive Oil
- 3 cloves Garlic, thinly sliced
- 1 tsp Chili Flakes (adjust to taste)
- Salt, to taste
- Lemon zest from 1 lemon
- 2 tbsp Nutritional Yeast (for a cheesy flavor)

TOTAL NUTRITIONAL VALUE

Calories: 2,150; Protein: 60g; Carbohydrates: 380g;
Fat: 40g; Fiber: 20g; Sugar: 6g

DIRECTIONS

1. Prepare the dough using the listed ingredients and shape into spaghetti following the step-by-step Directions.
2. In a large skillet, heat olive oil over medium heat. Add the thinly sliced garlic and sauté until it's fragrant but not browned.
3. Add the chopped broccoli rabe to the skillet. Cook, stirring occasionally, until the broccoli rabe is tender and slightly caramelized.
4. Stir in the chili flakes and season with salt. Add a bit of lemon zest for freshness.
5. Bring a large pot of salted water to boil. Add the spaghetti and cook until al dente. Reserve 1/2 cup of pasta water and then drain the pasta.
6. Add the drained spaghetti to the skillet with the broccoli rabe. Toss to combine, adding reserved pasta water a little at a time if needed to help the sauce cling to the pasta.
7. Serve immediately, sprinkled with nutritional yeast for a cheesy flavor.

VEGAN SPAGHETTI WITH CREAMY CASHEW AND ROASTED RED PEPPER SAUCE

SERVES: 4-6 PREP: 20 min COOK: 15 min
(plus soaking time for cashews)

INGREDIENTS

For the Dough:
- 150 g "Tipo 00" Flour or all-purpose flour
- 150 g semolina flour (or substitute with more regular flour)
- ½ tsp salt
- 150 ml water (room temperature)
- 2 tsp olive oil

For the Seasoning:
- 1 cup (150g) Raw Cashews, soaked for 4 hours or overnight, then drained
- 2 Roasted Red Peppers (from a jar or freshly roasted)
- 2 cloves Garlic
- 1/4 cup (20g) Nutritional Yeast
- 1/2 cup (120g) Water or Unsweetened Almond Milk
- 2 tbsp Olive Oil
- 1 tsp Smoked Paprika
- Salt, to taste
- Fresh Basil, for garnish
- Crushed Red Pepper Flakes, for garnish (optional)

TOTAL NUTRITIONAL VALUE

Calories: 2,300; Protein: 70g; Carbohydrates: 340g;
Fat: 80g; Fiber: 18g; Sugar: 12g;

DIRECTIONS

1. Prepare the dough using the listed ingredients and shape into spaghetti following the step-by-step Directions.
2. In a blender, combine the soaked and drained cashews, roasted red peppers, garlic, nutritional yeast, water or almond milk, olive oil, smoked paprika, and salt. Blend until smooth and creamy. If the sauce is too thick, add a bit more water or almond milk to reach your desired consistency.
3. In a large skillet, warm the sauce over medium heat, stirring occasionally.
4. Bring a large pot of salted water to boil. Add the spaghetti and cook until al dente. Reserve 1/2 cup of pasta water and then drain the pasta.
5. Add the drained spaghetti to the skillet with the creamy cashew sauce. Toss to combine, adding reserved pasta water a little at a time if needed to help the sauce cling to the pasta.
6. Serve immediately, garnished with fresh basil and a sprinkle of crushed red pepper flakes if desired.

NOTE

The creamy cashew sauce provides a rich texture without the need for dairy. Adjust the amount of smoked paprika based on your preference. If you're in a hurry, you can use quick-soak method for cashews: boil them for 15 minutes.

VEGAN TAGLIATELLE WITH ARTICHOKES AND LEMON HERB SAUCE

SERVES: 4-6   PREP: 20 min   COOK: 25 min

INGREDIENTS

For the Dough:
- 150 g "Tipo 00" Flour or all-purpose flour
- 150 g semolina flour (or substitute with more regular flour)
- ½ tsp salt
- 150 ml water (room temperature)
- 2 tsp olive oil

For the Seasoning:
- 1 can (14 oz or 400g) artichoke hearts, drained and quartered
- Zest and juice of 1 lemon
- 3 cloves garlic, minced
- 1/4 cup (60 ml) extra virgin olive oil
- 1/4 cup (15g) fresh parsley, chopped
- 1/4 cup (15g) fresh basil, chopped
- Salt and pepper to taste
- Red pepper flakes (optional)
- 1/4 cup (20g) vegan Parmesan cheese or nutritional yeast, for serving

DIRECTIONS

1. Prepare the dough using the listed ingredients and shape into tagliatelle following the step-by-step Directions.
2. In a large skillet, heat the olive oil over medium heat. Add the minced garlic and sauté until fragrant, about 1 minute.
3. Add the artichoke hearts to the skillet and sauté for 5-7 minutes until they start to brown.
4. Stir in the lemon zest, lemon juice, parsley, and basil. Season with salt, pepper, and red pepper flakes if using. Cook for another 2-3 minutes.
5. Meanwhile, cook the tagliatelle in a large pot of boiling salted water until al dente. Drain and add to the skillet with the artichoke and herb sauce.
6. Toss the pasta well to coat with the sauce. Serve hot, garnished with vegan Parmesan cheese or nutritional yeast.

TOTAL NUTRITIONAL VALUE

Calories: 2,100; Protein: 60g; Carbohydrates: 340g; Fat: 60g; Fiber: 18g; Sugar: 10g

VEGAN TAGLIATELLE WITH ROASTED BEETROOT AND SPINACH PESTO

SERVES: 4-6   PREP: 25 min   COOK: 45 min

INGREDIENTS

For the Dough:
- 150 g "Tipo 00" Flour or all-purpose flour
- 150 g semolina flour (or substitute with more regular flour)
- ½ tsp salt
- 150 ml water (room temperature)
- 2 tsp olive oil

For the Seasoning:
- 2 medium beetroots, peeled and diced
- 2 cups (60-70g) fresh spinach
- 1/4 cup (30-40g) walnuts or pine nuts
- 3 cloves garlic
- 1/4 cup (60 ml) extra virgin olive oil, plus more for roasting
- Salt and pepper to taste
- Juice of 1/2 lemon
- 1/4 cup (20g) vegan Parmesan cheese or nutritional yeast, for serving

DIRECTIONS

1. Prepare the dough using the listed ingredients and shape into tagliatelle following the step-by-step Directions.
2. Preheat the oven to 400°F (200°C). Toss the diced beetroots with a drizzle of olive oil, salt, and pepper. Spread them out on a baking sheet and roast for 25-30 minutes or until tender.
3. In a food processor, combine the roasted beetroots, spinach, walnuts or pine nuts, garlic, olive oil, and lemon juice. Blend until smooth. Season with salt and pepper to taste.
4. Meanwhile, cook the tagliatelle in a large pot of boiling salted water until al dente. Drain and return to the pot.
5. Pour the beetroot and spinach pesto over the tagliatelle and toss to combine. Serve hot, garnished with vegan Parmesan cheese or nutritional yeast.

NOTE

Roasting the beetroots enhances their natural sweetness, which pairs beautifully with the earthy spinach.

TOTAL NUTRITIONAL VALUE

Calories: 2,250; Protein: 65g; Carbohydrates: 360g; Fat: 70g; Fiber: 20g; Sugar: 14g

VEGAN FETTUCCINE WITH ASPARAGUS AND LEMON-PEPPER SAUCE

SERVES: 4-6   PREP: 20 min   COOK: 25 min

INGREDIENTS

For the Dough:
- 150 g "Tipo 00" Flour or all-purpose flour
- 150 g semolina flour
- ½ tsp salt
- 150 ml water (room temperature)
- 2 tsp olive oil

For the Seasoning:
- 1 bunch of asparagus, trimmed and cut into 2-inch pieces
- Zest and juice of 1 lemon
- 3 garlic cloves, minced
- 1/4 cup (60g) extra virgin olive oil
- Salt and freshly ground black pepper, to taste
- Fresh parsley, chopped, for garnish
- Vegan Parmesan cheese or nutritional yeast, for serving

DIRECTIONS

1. Prepare the dough using the listed ingredients and shape into fettuccine following the step-by-step Directions.
2. In a large skillet, heat olive oil over medium heat. Add the minced garlic and sauté until fragrant.
3. Add the asparagus to the skillet and cook until tender but still crisp.
4. Stir in the lemon zest and juice, then season with salt and freshly ground black pepper.
5. Meanwhile, cook the fettuccine in a large pot of boiling salted water until al dente. Before draining the pasta, reserve about 1/2 cup (120 ml) of the cooking water.
6. Drain the fettuccine and add to the skillet with the asparagus. If the mixture is too dry or if you desire a glossier sauce, gradually add the reserved cooking water until you reach the desired consistency.
7. Season again if needed. Serve garnished with chopped fresh parsley and vegan Parmesan cheese or a sprinkle of nutritional yeast.

TOTAL NUTRITIONAL VALUE

Calories: 1,800; Protein: 60g; Carbohydrates: 290g; Fat: 40g; Fiber: 12g; Sugar: 6g

NOTE

Asparagus is best enjoyed when it's in season, typically in the spring. For an added touch of richness, you can top the dish with some toasted pine nuts.

VEGAN FETTUCCINE WITH EGGPLANT AND TOMATO RAGÙ

SERVES: 4-6   PREP: 25 min   COOK: 35 min

INGREDIENTS

For the Dough:
- 150 g "Tipo 00" Flour or all-purpose flour
- 150 g semolina flour
- ½ tsp salt
- 150 ml water (room temperature)
- 2 tsp olive oil

For the Seasoning:
- 1 large eggplant, diced into 1/2-inch cubes
- 1 can (28 oz or 800g) crushed tomatoes
- 3 garlic cloves, minced
- 1/4 cup (60g) extra virgin olive oil
- Salt and freshly ground black pepper, to taste
- Fresh basil, chopped, for garnish
- Vegan Parmesan cheese or nutritional yeast, for serving

DIRECTIONS

1. Prepare the dough using the listed ingredients and shape into fettuccine following the step-by-step Directions.
2. In a large skillet, heat olive oil over medium heat. Add the minced garlic and sauté until fragrant.
3. Add the diced eggplant to the skillet and cook until it starts to soften and brown.
4. Pour in the crushed tomatoes and season with salt and freshly ground black pepper. Let the sauce simmer for about 20 minutes, allowing the flavors to meld.
5. Meanwhile, cook the fettuccine in a large pot of boiling salted water until al dente. Before draining the pasta, reserve about 1/2 cup (120 ml) of the cooking water.
6. Drain the fettuccine and add to the skillet with the eggplant and tomato ragù. If the mixture is too thick, gradually add the reserved cooking water until you reach the desired consistency.
7. Season again if needed. Serve garnished with chopped fresh basil and vegan Parmesan cheese or a sprinkle of nutritional yeast.

TOTAL NUTRITIONAL VALUE

Calories: 1,900; Protein: 65g; Carbohydrates: 310g; Fat: 45g; Fiber: 15g; Sugar: 14g

NOTE

Eggplants absorb a lot of oil when cooked. To reduce the amount of oil absorbed, you can salt the diced eggplant and let it sit for about 30 minutes before rinsing and cooking. This will draw out some of the moisture and make the eggplant less sponge-like.

VEGAN PAPPARDELLE WITH BRAISED LENTILS AND KALE

SERVES: 4-6 PREP: 25 min COOK: 40 min

INGREDIENTS

For the Dough:
- 150 g "Tipo 00" Flour or all-purpose flour
- 150 g semolina flour
- ½ tsp salt
- 150 ml water (room temperature)
- 2 tsp olive oil

For the Seasoning:
- 1 cup (200g) green lentils, rinsed and drained
- 2 cups (134g) kale, stems removed and roughly chopped
- 3 garlic cloves, minced
- 1/4 cup (60 ml) extra virgin olive oil
- 1 onion, finely chopped
- 2 cups (480 ml) vegetable broth
- Salt and freshly ground black pepper, to taste
- Fresh parsley, chopped, for garnish
- Vegan Parmesan cheese or nutritional yeast, for serving

DIRECTIONS

1. Prepare the dough using the listed ingredients and shape into pappardelle following the step-by-step Directions.
2. In a large skillet, heat olive oil over medium heat. Add the finely chopped onion and sauté until translucent.
3. Add the minced garlic and sauté until fragrant.
4. Add the lentils and vegetable broth to the skillet. Bring to a boil, then reduce heat and let simmer until lentils are tender, about 25-30 minutes.
5. Stir in the chopped kale and cook until wilted.
6. Meanwhile, cook the pappardelle in a large pot of boiling salted water until al dente. Before draining the pasta, reserve about 1/2 cup (120 ml) of the cooking water.
7. Drain the pappardelle and add to the skillet with the lentil and kale mixture. Toss well to combine. If the mixture is too dry, gradually add the reserved cooking water until you reach the desired consistency.
8. Season with salt and pepper. Serve garnished with chopped fresh parsley and a sprinkle of vegan Parmesan cheese or nutritional yeast.

TOTAL NUTRITIONAL VALUE

Calories: 1,850; Protein: 70g; Carbohydrates: 310g;
Fat: 40g; Fiber: 20g; Sugar: 8g

VEGAN PAPPARDELLE WITH ROASTED BUTTERNUT SQUASH AND SAGE

SERVES: 4-6 PREP: 30 min COOK: 45 min

INGREDIENTS

For the Dough:
- 150 g "Tipo 00" Flour or all-purpose flour
- 150 g semolina flour
- ½ tsp salt
- 150 ml water (room temperature)
- 2 tsp olive oil

For the Seasoning:
- 1 medium butternut squash, peeled, seeded, and diced
- 2 tbsp (30g) seed oil
- 1/4 cup (60g) extra virgin olive oil
- 10 fresh sage leaves
- 3 garlic cloves, minced
- Salt and freshly ground black pepper, to taste
- Fresh parsley, chopped, for garnish
- Vegan Parmesan cheese or nutritional yeast, for serving

DIRECTIONS

1. Prepare the dough using the listed ingredients and shape into pappardelle following the step-by-step Directions.
2. Preheat the oven to 400°F (200°C). Toss the diced butternut squash with 2 tbsp of seed oil, salt, and pepper. Spread on a baking sheet and roast for 25-30 minutes or until tender and slightly caramelized.
3. In a large skillet, heat 1/4 cup of olive oil over medium heat. Add the sage leaves and fry until crispy. Remove the sage leaves and set aside.
4. Add the minced garlic to the skillet and sauté until fragrant.
5. Add the roasted butternut squash to the skillet and toss to combine.
6. Meanwhile, cook the pappardelle in a large pot of boiling salted water until al dente. Before draining the pasta, reserve about 1/2 cup (120 ml) of the cooking water.
7. Drain the pappardelle and add to the skillet with the butternut squash mixture. Toss well to combine. If the mixture is too dry, gradually add the reserved cooking water until you reach the desired consistency.
8. Season with salt and pepper. Serve garnished with the crispy sage leaves, chopped fresh parsley, and a sprinkle of vegan Parmesan cheese or nutritional yeast.

TOTAL NUTRITIONAL VALUE

Calories: 1,900; Protein: 55g; Carbohydrates: 320g;
Fat: 45g; Fiber: 15g; Sugar: 10g

VEGAN LASAGNE WITH SPINACH, TOFU RICOTTA, AND CASHEW BECHAMEL

SERVES: 6-8   PREP: 60 min   COOK: 60 min

INGREDIENTS

For the Dough:
- 150 g "Tipo 00" Flour or all-purpose flour
- 150 g semolina flour
- ½ tsp salt
- 150 ml water (room temperature)
- 2 tsp olive oil

For the Seasoning:
- 3 cups (220g) fresh spinach, chopped
- 1 block (14 oz or 400g) firm tofu, drained and crumbled
- 2 cups (450/500g) cashew béchamel (blend 1 cup soaked cashews, 2 cups water, 2 tbsp nutritional yeast, 1 garlic clove, salt, and pepper until smooth)
- 1/4 cup (60g) extra virgin olive oil
- 3 garlic cloves, minced
- Salt and freshly ground black pepper, to taste
- Fresh basil, for garnish

TOTAL NUTRITIONAL VALUE

Calories: 3,500; Protein: 120g; Carbohydrates: 380g; Fat: 180g; Fiber: 25g; Sugar: 15g

DIRECTIONS

1. Prepare the dough using the listed ingredients and shape into lasagna noodles following the step-by-step Directions. Given the creamy nature of cashew béchamel, there's no need to pre-cook the noodles.
2. In a skillet, heat olive oil over medium heat. Add the minced garlic and sauté until fragrant. Add the chopped spinach and cook until wilted. Remove from heat and let cool.
3. In a mixing bowl, combine the crumbled tofu, sautéed spinach, salt, and pepper to create the tofu ricotta mixture.
4. Preheat your oven to 375°F (190°C).
5. Assemble the lasagna in a 9x13" baking dish by spreading a thin layer of cashew béchamel at the bottom. Place a layer of lasagna noodles over the sauce. Spread a layer of tofu ricotta, followed by more cashew béchamel. Repeat layers until all ingredients are used, finishing with a layer of cashew béchamel on top.
6. Cover with aluminum foil and bake for 40 minutes. Remove foil and bake for an additional 20 minutes, or until bubbly and golden.
7. Let it rest for at least 15 minutes before serving. Garnish with fresh basil before serving.

VEGAN LASAGNE WITH EGGPLANT, ZUCCHINI, AND TOMATO BASIL SAUCE

SERVES: 6-8   PREP: 50 min   COOK: 60 min

INGREDIENTS

For the Dough:
- 150 g "Tipo 00" Flour or all-purpose flour
- 150 g semolina flour
- ½ tsp salt
- 150 ml water (room temperature)
- 2 tsp olive oil

For the Seasoning:
- 1 large eggplant, thinly sliced
- 2 zucchinis, thinly sliced
- 3 cups (700g) tomato basil sauce (look at Green Spinach Capellini recipe)
- 1/4 cup (60g) extra virgin olive oil
- Salt and freshly ground black pepper, to taste
- Fresh basil, for garnish
- Vegan Parmesan cheese or nutritional yeast, for serving

DIRECTIONS

1. Prepare the dough using the listed ingredients and shape into lasagna noodles following the step-by-step Directions. Given the moisture from the vegetables and sauce, there's no need to pre-cook the noodles.
2. Preheat your oven to 400°F (200°C). Toss the sliced eggplant and zucchini in olive oil, salt, and pepper. Spread them out on a baking sheet and roast for 20-25 minutes or until tender.
3. Reduce the oven temperature to 375°F (190°C).
4. Assemble the lasagna in a 9x13" baking dish by spreading a thin layer of tomato basil sauce at the bottom. Place a layer of lasagna noodles over the sauce. Add a layer of roasted vegetables, followed by more tomato basil sauce. Repeat layers until all ingredients are used, finishing with a layer of tomato basil sauce on top.
5. Cover with aluminum foil and bake for 40 minutes. Remove foil and bake for an additional 20 minutes, or until bubbly and golden.
6. Let it rest for at least 15 minutes before serving. Garnish with fresh basil and a sprinkle of vegan Parmesan cheese or nutritional yeast.

TOTAL NUTRITIONAL VALUE

Calories: 2,800; Protein: 80g; Carbohydrates: 400g; Fat: 80g; Fiber: 30g; Sugar: 25g

NOTE

Roasting the eggplant and zucchini enhances their flavors and ensures they don't release too much moisture into the lasagna. If you prefer a richer taste, consider adding a layer of vegan mozzarella or cashew ricotta.

VEGAN RAVIOLI WITH SWEET POTATO AND ROSEMARY FILLING

SERVES: 16-32   PREP: 50 min   COOK: 25 min

INGREDIENTS

For the Dough:
- 150 g "Tipo 00" Flour or all-purpose flour
- 150 g semolina flour
- ½ tsp salt
- 150 ml water (room temperature)
- 2 tsp olive oil

For the Filling:
- 2 medium sweet potatoes (about 1 lb or 450g total)
- 1 tablespoon fresh rosemary, finely chopped
- Salt and pepper, to taste
- Olive oil, for roasting
- For the Sauce:
- 1/4 cup (60 ml) extra virgin olive oil
- 2 garlic cloves, minced
- Fresh rosemary sprigs
- Salt and pepper, to taste
- Chopped fresh parsley, for garnish

TOTAL NUTRITIONAL VALUE

Calories: 2,100; Protein: 40g; Carbohydrates: 380g;

Fat: 50g; Fiber: 20g; Sugar: 15g

DIRECTIONS

1. Prepare the dough using the listed ingredients and create a ravioli sheet following the step-by-step Directions.
2. For the filling, preheat the oven to 400°F (200°C). Halve the sweet potatoes and brush the cut sides with olive oil. Place them cut side down on a baking sheet and roast for 25-30 minutes or until tender. Once cooled, scoop out the flesh and mash it in a bowl. Mix in the finely chopped rosemary, salt, and pepper.
3. Fill each ravioli with a spoonful of the sweet potato mixture and seal them following the Directions. given in the ravioli chapter.
4. In a skillet over medium heat, warm the olive oil. Add the minced garlic and rosemary sprigs, sautéing until fragrant.
5. Cook the ravioli in batches (8 at a time) until they float to the top.
6. Gently toss the cooked ravioli in the garlic-rosemary olive oil.
7. Serve garnished with chopped fresh parsley.

NOTE

If you desire a richer sauce, consider adding a splash of coconut milk to the skillet.

VEGAN RAVIOLI WITH MUSHROOM AND WALNUT FILLING

SERVES: 16-32   PREP: 55 min   COOK: 30 min

INGREDIENTS

For the Dough:
- 150 g "Tipo 00" Flour or all-purpose flour
- 150 g semolina flour
- ½ tsp salt
- 150 ml water (room temperature)
- 2 tsp olive oil

For the Filling:
- 2 cups (about 200g) mushrooms, finely chopped
- 1/2 cup (60g) walnuts, finely chopped
- 1 small onion, finely diced
- 2 garlic cloves, minced
- 2 tbsp olive oil
- Salt and pepper, to taste

For the Sauce:
- 1/4 cup (60 ml) extra virgin olive oil
- 2 garlic cloves, minced
- Fresh thyme sprigs
- Salt and pepper, to taste
- Vegan Parmesan cheese or nutritional yeast, for serving

TOTAL NUTRITIONAL VALUE

Calories: 2,300; Protein: 60g; Carbohydrates: 390g;

Fat: 70g; Fiber: 25g; Sugar: 10g

DIRECTIONS

1. Prepare the dough using the listed ingredients and create a ravioli sheet following the step-by-step Directions.
2. For the filling, in a skillet over medium heat, warm the olive oil. Add the onion and garlic, sautéing until translucent. Add the mushrooms and cook until they release their moisture and become golden. Stir in the finely chopped walnuts, salt, and pepper. Remove from heat and let the mixture cool.
3. Fill each ravioli with a spoonful of the mushroom-walnut mixture and seal them following the Directions. given in the ravioli chapter.
4. In a skillet over medium heat, warm the olive oil. Add the minced garlic and thyme sprigs, sautéing until fragrant.
5. Cook the ravioli in batches (8 at a time) until they float to the top.
6. Gently toss the cooked ravioli in the garlic-thyme olive oil.
7. Serve sprinkled with vegan Parmesan cheese or nutritional yeast.

NOTE

If you want a creamier sauce, consider adding a splash of almond or soy milk to the skillet.

VEGAN CAPELLINI WITH ROASTED GARLIC AND CHERRY TOMATO SAUCE

SERVES: 4-6   PREP: 20 min   COOK: 30 min

INGREDIENTS

For the Dough:
- 150 g "Tipo 00" Flour or all-purpose flour
- 150 g semolina flour
- ½ tsp salt
- 150 ml water (room temperature)
- 2 tsp olive oil

For the Seasoning:
- 2 cups (about 300g) cherry tomatoes, halved
- 6 garlic cloves, left whole with skin on
- 1/4 cup (60 ml) extra virgin olive oil, plus more for drizzling
- Salt and freshly ground black pepper, to taste
- Fresh basil leaves, for garnish

TOTAL NUTRITIONAL VALUE

Calories: 1,900; Protein: 50g; Carbohydrates: 340g; Fat: 40g; Fiber: 15g; Sugar: 12g;

DIRECTIONS

1. Prepare the dough using the listed ingredients and shape into capellini following the step-by-step Directions.
2. Preheat the oven to 425°F (220°C). Toss the cherry tomatoes and whole garlic cloves with olive oil, salt, and pepper. Spread on a baking sheet and roast for 20-25 minutes, or until tomatoes are soft and slightly caramelized.
3. Once the tomatoes and garlic are roasted, remove from the oven and let cool slightly. Squeeze the roasted garlic out of its skin and mash it with a fork. Mix it with the roasted tomatoes to form a sauce.
4. In a large skillet, heat a bit more olive oil over medium heat. Add the tomato-garlic mixture and sauté for a few minutes to combine flavors.
5. Meanwhile, cook the capellini in a large pot of boiling salted water until al dente. Before draining the pasta, reserve about 1/2 cup (120 ml) of the cooking water.
6. Drain the capellini and add to the skillet with the tomato-garlic sauce. Toss to combine. If the mixture is too dry or if you desire a glossier sauce, gradually add the reserved cooking water until you reach the desired consistency.
7. Season with additional salt and pepper if needed. Serve garnished with fresh basil leaves.

VEGAN CAPELLINI WITH ARUGULA AND OLIVE TAPENADE

SERVES: 4-6   PREP: 20 min   COOK: 15 min

INGREDIENTS

For the Dough:
- 150 g "Tipo 00" Flour or all-purpose flour
- 150 g semolina flour
- ½ tsp salt
- 150 ml water (room temperature)
- 2 tsp olive oil

For the Seasoning:
- 1 cup (about 150g) pitted black olives
- 1/4 cup (60 ml) extra virgin olive oil
- 2 garlic cloves
- 1 cup (about 20g) fresh arugula
- Zest of 1 lemon
- Salt and freshly ground black pepper, to taste

DIRECTIONS

1. Prepare the dough using the listed ingredients and shape into capellini following the step-by-step Directions.
2. In a food processor, combine the olives, olive oil, and garlic. Blend until you get a smooth tapenade consistency. Stir in the lemon zest and set aside.
3. Cook the capellini in a large pot of boiling salted water until al dente. Before draining the pasta, reserve about 1/2 cup (120 ml) of the cooking water.
4. Drain the capellini and return them to the pot. Add the olive tapenade and toss to coat the pasta evenly. If the mixture is too dry, gradually add the reserved cooking water until you reach the desired consistency.
5. Season with salt and pepper. Serve the pasta on plates and top with fresh arugula.

TOTAL NUTRITIONAL VALUE

Calories: 1,850; Protein: 45g; Carbohydrates: 330g; Fat: 50g; Fiber: 12g; Sugar: 5g

CONCLUSION

Ah, dear ones, as we come to the end of this delightful journey through the world of pasta, I can't help but feel a warmth in my heart. It's the same warmth I feel every time I gather my family around the dinner table, serving them dishes that have been passed down through generations.

You see, pasta is more than just a dish; it's a tapestry of memories, traditions, and love. Every strand of spaghetti, every fold of ravioli, tells a story. And now, you too are a part of this grand narrative.

I remember, many moons ago, when I first tried my hand at making pasta. It wasn't perfect, and I had flour everywhere! But with each attempt, I got better, and soon, I was crafting dishes that would make my Nonna proud. I share this with you to remind you that it's okay if things don't turn out perfect the first time. As I always say, "If it doesn't turn out right the first time, that's just an opportunity to try again." And trust me, the joy of finally getting it right is unparalleled.

Now, let's take a pause to consider the vast world of pasta we've explored. From the classic spaghetti to the intricate ravioli, we've journeyed through the heart of Italian cuisine. And while we've covered a lot, remember that the world of pasta is as vast as the Italian coastline. There's always more to discover, more to taste, and more to create.

Kneading the dough, shaping it, and cooking it is like dancing to a song that's been sung for centuries. And every time you make pasta, you add your own verse to this age-old melody.

In conclusion, I want to leave you with a thought. Cooking, especially pasta, is an act of love. It's a way to connect with your roots, with your family, and with yourself. So, the next time you're in the kitchen, remember to pour your heart into every dish. Because, as we've learned, pasta is not just about the ingredients; it's about the love and passion you put into it.

I truly hope you've found this book helpful and enlightening. If you did, I'd be ever so grateful if you could leave an honest review. Your feedback is invaluable and greatly supports my work. Grazie mille for joining me on this journey. Until next time, buon appetito!

RECIPE INDEX

HERE'S A SNEAK PEEK OF WHAT YOU'LL DISCOVER:

🎁**Beyond the Machine**🎁 Learn how to make over 10 Unique Handmade Pasta Shapes like orecchiette, pici and cavatelli with step-by-step illustrated guide

🎁 **Pasta Machine Hacks** 🎁 9 surprising uses you've never tried to unlock the full potential of your Pasta Maker!

Made in the USA
Las Vegas, NV
17 September 2024